THE NUMERACY TEST WORKBOOK

THE NUMERACY TEST WORKBOOK

INTERMEDIATE LEVEl

MIKE BRYON

KOGAN PAGE

Publisher's Note

Every possible effort has been made to ensure that the information contained in this book is accurate at the time of going to press, and the publishers and authors cannot accept responsibility for any errors or omissions, however caused. No responsibility for loss or damage occasioned to any person acting, or refraining from action, as a result of the material in this publication can be accepted by the editor, the publisher or any of the authors.

First Indian Edition 2008

Kogan Page India Private Limited
4737/23 Ansari Road,
Daryaganj
New Delhi 110 002

This edition is for sale in Indian subcontinent only. Not for export elsewhere.

ISBN-10: 81-7554-389-2
ISBN-13: 978-81-7554-389-8

Published by Vinod Vasishtha for Kogan Page India Private Limited, 4737/23 Ansari Road, Daryaganj, New Delhi 110 002.

Printed and bound at Anand Sons, Delhi - 110 092.

Contents

How to use this book *vii*

1 **Adopt the winning approach** 1
Great candidate except for the maths! 1
Everyone can pass 2
Put aside any feeling of resentment 2
The importance of practice 3
Get test wise 3
What to expect on the day 5

2 **Speed is of the essence** 7
Quick tests 8
Quick test 1 11
Quick test 2 15
Quick test 3 21
Quick test 4 29
Quick test 5 37

3 **The secrets of number sequencing revealed** 45
Sequencing 45
The first 40 questions 46
160 more number sequence questions 50

4	**Become brilliant at number problems**	**61**
	Forty questions that do *not* involve percentages but may require you to work fractions and ratios	62
	Introducing percentage number problems	68
	Forty-two more number problems	72
5	**Succeed in data interpretation tests**	**79**
	A hundred practice questions	79
6	**Practise under realistic test conditions to win**	**101**
	Test 1 Number problems	103
	Test 2 Sequencing	111
	Test 3 Data interpretation	117
	Answers and detailed explanations	**129**
	Chapter 2	129
	Chapter 3	152
	Chapter 4	173
	Chapter 5	188
	Chapter 6	203
	Interpretations of your scores	**220**
	Chapter 1 quick tests	220
	Realistic tests chapter 6	222

How to use this book

This book is the perfect starting point if you lack practice or confidence and face a numeracy test. It provides all you need to undertake a major programme of self-study and get some valuable test practice without the pressure of a job offer hinging on your performance. All you have to do is settle down somewhere quiet and get practising. Very soon you will be more confident, much faster at answering these types of question, and achieve a much higher score.

If you have always hated maths then now is the time to get down to some serious study and overcome your anxieties. To succeed you may need to work harder than some of your friends or colleagues, but if you let it take over your life for a while and really go for it, then you will triumph.

First make sure you adopt the winning mindset detailed in Chapter 1, and at the earliest opportunity find out about the type of questions that make up the test you face. Next, work through the key operations in Chapters 2 and 3. Allow yourself sufficient time to practise, especially on the bits of the test that represent the greatest challenge to you. Now get down to lots more score-improving practice on the realistic practice questions provided in Chapters 4 and 5. Finally, practise under realistic test conditions on the practice tests in Chapter 6. As you go along check your answers, review the explanations and interpret your scores in the last two chapters of the book.

I have signposted sources of further practice available in the Kogan Page Testing Series so that you can continue your programme of revision and prepare for all types of tests and all levels of difficulty.

Each chapter starts with easier material and gets progressively harder. You will find therefore that the questions in an actual test are more difficult than the questions at the beginning of each chapter. This is intentional as it helps to ensure that you build up to the level required to do well in a numeracy test at the intermediate level.

I have set all questions which require you to calculate a value in dollars ($). You can take this to relate to any one of the world's many dollar currencies, and you are not required to calculate in cents. Some questions require you to calculate quantities, and in almost every instance I have adopted the metric system.

If you face a test that contains questions of a type not covered by this title or the suggested further reading, then by all means contact me care of Kogan Page, and if I know of one I will be glad to tell you about a source of suitable practice material.

May I apologize in advance if you find an error in this book. I have worked hard to keep them out. Please do not let any undermine your belief in the value of practice, and do please take the trouble to notify me, care of Kogan Page, so that it can be removed at the next reprint.

Mike Bryon

1

Adopt the winning approach

Great candidate except for the maths!

This book is intended for the reader who faces a test of numeracy and who lacks either practice or confidence in those fundamental skills. If the maths classes of school are a distant or bad memory, if numerical skills are something you have so far managed without, then this is the book for you. It will not suit the reader preparing for advanced numeracy tests.

We face tests at so many points in our career, at school obviously but increasingly when we apply for jobs or courses, and in work when, for example, we apply for promotion or a career move. Employers and course administrators are looking for all-round candidates, those with a balanced set of essential skills including numeracy skills. Tests are used to distinguish between the candidates with and without these skills, and tests of numeracy are one of the most common types. You will come across a numeracy paper in most tests in use today.

It does not matter that you perform well in other subject areas. You might for example have very strong verbal skills, and you will no doubt be given the opportunity to demonstrate these in another part of the assessment. But to guarantee success you have to pass all the subtests that make up the assessment. If you neglect the numeracy test hoping to rely on a high score in your area of personal strength, you run the risk of being rejected as a great candidate except for the maths!

Everyone can pass

The good news is that you will pass these tests if you make the necessary commitment. It takes some people longer than others to reach that point. Some candidates have to work much harder, but that goes for most things in life. We all have our personal strengths and challenges. To succeed you need time, determination and hard work. To master these skills, to make the necessary commitment, can be really boring, painful even, but if success is important then you have no real alternative but to get on with it.

Put aside any feeling of resentment

Perhaps you know that you can do the job and therefore naturally ask yourself, why do they insist on my having to pass this silly test? You might wonder what relevance the test has to the role for which you have applied. Many candidates raise the objection that in the job they will use a calculator or computer program to complete numerical tasks, so why do they have to pass a numeracy test without using these everyday office tools?

These are understandable and common sentiments. But you really must try to put them all aside as they are counterproductive and will serve only to distract you from the real task at hand: passing the test. To do this you have to adopt the right mental approach. If you turn up on the day harbouring resentments then you are unlikely to demonstrate your true potential. The winning candidate concentrates not on the threat or inconvenience, but instead on the opportunity the test represents. Pass it and you can go on to realize your personal goal. See the test as a chance to show how strong a candidate you really are. Attend fully prepared, with confidence in your own ability and ready to succeed. Realize that doing well in a test is not simply a matter of intelligence but also requires determination and hard work. If passing is important to you, be prepared to both set aside a significant number of hours in which to practise, and work very hard during the real test.

If you have faced failure in the past when you previously tried and failed to master these skills, then it will take courage to make the necessary commitment.

The importance of practice

You must seek to achieve the best possible score in the test. Other candidates will be trying to do this so you must too. The secret is practice. Everyone will improve their test score with practice, and for many candidates practice will mean the difference between pass and fail. Practice works best on material that is as much like the questions in the real test as possible. Revise the fundamental operations in Chapters 2 to 5 and select from Chapter 6 the practice tests that are most similar to the real test. Then sit these practice tests as if they were the real thing. Where necessary obtain further material from other titles in the Kogan Page testing series.

Practise right up to the day before the test. Practice, to be effective, must be challenging. To be sure that you are continuing to improve, make sure that the practice remains a challenge. If it stops being a pain then there really will be very little gain. But before you start practising, first you must get test wise.

Get test wise

As soon as you realize you need to pass a numeracy test, go about finding out as much as you can about it. The organization that has invited you should provide you with, or direct you to, a description of the test and some sample questions. You will not be able to get hold of past papers or real copies of the test.

Most tests comprise a series of smaller tests taken one after the other, with a short pause between the papers. They might include for example first a subtest on verbal reasoning, then a numerical reasoning subtest and finally a nonverbal reasoning subtest, but this is only one of many possible combinations. The series of subtests is called a battery. It is really important that you understand exactly what each part of the test involves. You would be astonished how many people attend for a test not knowing what to expect. The first time they learn of the type of questions is when the test administrator describes them just before the test begins for real. Don't make this mistake. You need to know the nature of the challenge as soon as possible. Get details on:

- how many subtests the test battery comprises;
- what the title of each subtest is;
- what sort of question makes up a subtest (find an example of each type of question);
- how many questions each subtest includes;
- how long you are allowed to complete each subtest;
- whether it is multiple choice or short answer;
- whether you complete it with pen and paper or at a computer terminal;
- whether or not a calculator is allowed.

Once you have a clear idea of the test you face, you need to set about finding hundreds of relevant practice questions. You need hundreds because if you are weak at maths then you will have to practise a lot. This book contains over 700 questions. In the Kogan Page series you will find complementary publications that offer lots more practice questions and alternative explanations of the key competencies. Use them to practise lots more, and to find the explanation that clicks with you. Also in the series are titles containing advance material on verbal tests and specialist titles intended for particular tests such as those for the police, fire service or UK Civil Service.

If you suffer from a disability that will adversely affect your ability to complete the test or any aspect of the recruitment process, inform the organization at the first opportunity. It should be prepared to organize things differently to better accommodate your needs, and for certain conditions it might allow extra time for you to complete the test.

After the test the organisation should be willing to provide information on your performance, although you might have to ask for it. It should indicate the areas in which you performed strongly and areas in which you might work to improve. Most will be willing to discuss your score with you over the telephone, and this is often the way to get the most valuable feedback.

What to expect on the day

It is most likely that you will be invited to attend a training or recruitment centre to take the test. Don't be late! And dress smartly. You are likely to be one of many candidates attending that day. You might be expected to attend for some hours, and it is possible that you will be required to complete a whole series of exercises. All this detail will be included in your letter of invitation, so read it carefully.

Turn up prepared to work very hard indeed. Remember that doing well in any test requires hard work and determination. If at the end of the day you do not feel completely exhausted, you might have not done yourself justice, so go for it.

Expect to attend on the day with the ability to adopt the right mental approach. Keep in mind the winning approach, and attend looking forward to the challenge and the opportunity it represents. You are there to demonstrate your abilities and prove to the organization that you are a suitable candidate. Attend the test fully prepared, having spent many hours practising, and having addressed any areas of weakness. Do not underestimate how long it can take to prepare for a test. Start as soon as you receive notice that you must attend.

It is really important that you listen carefully to the instructions provided before a test begins. You may well be feeling nervous, and this might affect your concentration, so make yourself focus on what is being said. Much of the information will be a repeat of the test description sent to you with the letter inviting you to the test, so read and reread this document before the day of the test.

Pay particular attention to instructions on how many questions there are in each subtest, and be sure you are familiar with the demands of each style of question. Look to see if at the bottom of the page it tells you to turn over. You would be surprised how many people reach the bottom of a page and wrongly conclude that they have reached the end of the questions. They stop working and wait, when they should be working away at the remaining questions.

Keep track of the time during the test, and manage how long you spend on any one question. You must keep going right up to the end. Aim to get right the balance between speed and accuracy. It is better that you risk getting some questions wrong but attempt every question, rather than double-check each answer and be told to stop because you have run out of time before you have finished. Practice can really help develop this skill.

If you hit a difficult section of questions, don't lose heart. Keep going – everyone gets some questions wrong. You might find that you come next to a section of questions in which you can excel.

If you do not know the answer to a question, educated guessing is well worth a try. If you are unsure of an answer to a multiple-choice question, look to the suggested answers and try to rule some out as definitely wrong. This way you can reduce the number of suggested answers from which to guess, and with luck increase your chances of guessing correctly.

2

Speed is of the essence

Success in numerical reasoning tests requires you to be well practised in mental, or what is sometimes called mechanical, maths. By working through this chapter you will revise the key operations including multiplication, division, fractions, decimals, percentages, ratios and units of measurement. Importantly, you will develop the essential speed and accuracy at answering these key components to so many numeracy questions.

Before you skip this chapter on the grounds that it's too simple or boring, let me stress again the importance of speed. You might be able to do these questions relaxing at home or on the train, taking your time and pausing whenever you wish, but can you do them quickly enough and get them all right when you are pressed for time, feeling nervous, thinking about another part of the question, and 30 minutes into a 40-minute test?

You are not normally allowed to use a calculator in these tests, and if passing is important, do not risk attending on the day until you can quickly and routinely get questions like these right without a calculator.

The questions below have been organized as a series of quick tests. Use them to become really fast at these fundamental operations. This ability will repay you handsomely in a real test. While other candidates are recalling their basic maths you will be performing the basic calculations almost on autopilot. You will gain important seconds, make fewer mistakes and be better able to focus on the questions and avoid the traps that test authors so like to set.

To reach the required speed some readers will only need to revise what they have not practised for a number of years. Unfortunately, you have to keep using your maths otherwise it becomes rusty. Get practising, and after a few hours' hard work you will notice the improvement. Keep practising and you will soon be back up to full speed.

If you have never been good at maths, you will obviously need to do more than revise what you have previously forgotten. Most of us learn these skills in our childhood, and we forget just how much time and effort we spent acquiring them. To become competent as an adult takes almost as much time and effort as it does for a child, and because of all the other demands on an adult's time it also requires a high level of determination. You will need to let maths become something of a preoccupation, and work at it in most of your spare time. You will also need more practice questions than are contained in this title.

Further practice at this level is available in the following Kogan Page titles: *How to Pass Numeracy Tests* by Harry Tolley and Ken Thomas, *How to Pass Numerical Reasoning Tests* by Heidi Smith, and *How to Pass Selection Tests* by Mike Bryon and Sanjay Modha. If you would like to practise this sort of question on a computer, try the Kogan Page CD-ROM *Psychometric Tests Volume 1*, published in 2002.

Quick tests

As already mentioned, this chapter is organized as a series of quick tests. It contains 270 questions. Answers and explanations are provided from page 129. The first test is 30 questions long, and the remaining four tests contain 60 questions. I suggest that you start by allowing yourself 10 seconds a question. Readers who face challenging tests such as the SHL graduate battery of tests or the Civil Service fast stream should work towards being able to answer the majority of these questions in five seconds.

These tests will really help you to develop the speed and confidence necessary to do well in numeracy tests at any level. They will also help you develop a good exam technique and the flexibility of mind to switch between question types. Finally, they will help you develop the required stamina and endurance to battle through a long and demanding test.

The time limits are recommendations only. If you really are struggling with your maths and it better suits your circumstances, feel free to complete the questions without keeping track of the time, or adjust the time so that you allow yourself longer. Remember, however, that to do really well in a numeracy test you should keep practising until you can answer these questions in the recommended time. Use the interpretations of your scores to better understand what you need to do to succeed, and to identify sources of further practice.

Once you have completed a test, mark it and read the interpretation of your score. Spend some time going over the questions that you got wrong. Be honest with yourself, and if you did not do well because for example you do not know your multiplication tables, before you take the next quick test spend some time practising them. That way you will really see your score improve.

Good luck, and remember that to do well in a test you have to try really hard.

Quick test 1

Test instructions

Recommended time: five minutes to complete these 30 questions. That's 10 seconds a question.

You need to be able to answer these fundamental questions correctly but also quickly. In a real test you might be suffering from nerves, and are very likely to find yourself short of time. You need to be able to recognize the task when it is described in a confusing or unusual way. The more familiar you are with this sort of question, the fewer mistakes you will make when under real pressure in a real test. You should aim to be able to answer these questions almost automatically, and the only way you are likely to achieve this is through lots of practice.

Find a quiet comfortable place where you will not be interrupted, and using a stopwatch (many mobile phones have such a feature) or a watch with a second hand, prepare yourself for the quick test.

Some questions are multiple-choice, where you have to choose which is correct from one of the suggested answers. Others are short answer, where you have to write your answer in the box provided.

You will need a pencil to write down the answers but do not use a calculator.

Do not turn over the page until you are ready to begin.

Q1 13 x 5 = **Answer** ☐

Q2 117 – 21 = **Answer** ☐

Q3 80 + 75 = **Answer** ☐

Q4 7 x 11 = **Answer** ☐

Q5 83 – 16 = **Answer** ☐

Q6 20% is more than 1/8 (True or False) **Answer** ☐

Q7 16 + 18 = **Answer** ☐

Q8 8 x 8 = **Answer** ☐

Q9 1/4 is less than the ratio 1: 3 (True or False) **Answer** ☐

Q10 27 – 9 = **Answer** ☐

Q11 18% is more or less than 1 in 4 (More or Less) **Answer** ☐

Q12 94 + 15 = **Answer** ☐

Q13 13 x 9 = **Answer** ☐

Q14 209 – 81 = **Answer** ☐

Q15 13 + 78 = **Answer** ☐

Q16 6/20 is more than 30% (True or False) **Answer** ☐

Q17 6 x 7 = **Answer** ☐

Q18 77 – 42 = **Answer** ☐

Q19 18/24 is the same as 6/8 (True or False) **Answer** ☐

Q20 0.05 is the same as 5% (True or False) **Answer** ☐

Q21 9 x 9 = **Answer** ☐

Q22 96 + 97 = **Answer** ☐

Q23 300 – 119 = **Answer** ☐

Q24 Convert 1/5 into a decimal **Answer** ☐

Q25 15 x 3 = **Answer** ☐

Q26 27 – 16 = **Answer** ☐

Q27 2799 + 400 = **Answer** ☐

Q28 4 x 7 = **Answer** ☐

Q29 2000 – 390 = **Answer** ☐

Q30 6 x 5 = **Answer** ☐

End of the test

Quick test 2

Test instructions

This test comprises 60 questions and you are allowed 10 minutes in which to complete them.

The more you practise, the faster and more confident you will become in these key operations. Remember in a real test you might be suffering from nerves and are very likely to find yourself short of time. The more familiar you are with this sort of question, the fewer mistakes you will make when under pressure in a real test.

Find a quiet comfortable place where you will not be interrupted, and use a stopwatch or the stopwatch function on a mobile phone to time yourself exactly.

You will need a pencil to write down the answers, but do not use a calculator.

Do not turn the page until you are ready to begin.

Q1	28 + 109 =	**Answer**	
Q2	20% of 60 is	**Answer**	
Q3	21 – 8 =	**Answer**	
Q4	12.5% expressed as a fraction is 1/8 (True or False)	**Answer**	
Q5	5 x 7 =	**Answer**	
Q6	12/15 is equivalent to 3/4 (True or False)	**Answer**	
Q7	77 – 32 =	**Answer**	
Q8	66 + 87 =	**Answer**	
Q9	12 x 24 =	**Answer**	
Q10	12/5 is greater than 8/3 (True or False)	**Answer**	
Q11	4 x 9 =	**Answer**	
Q12	45 – 22 =	**Answer**	
Q13	What is the decimal 0.475 expressed as a percentage?	**Answer**	
Q14	6 x 12 =	**Answer**	
Q15	What is the decimal 0.4 expressed as an equivalent fraction (in its simplest form)?	**Answer**	
Q16	216 + 58 =	**Answer**	

Q17 14 x 8 = **Answer** ☐

Q18 Convert 3/5 into a percentage **Answer** ☐

Q19 Convert the fraction 3/4 into its equivalent percentage **Answer** ☐

Q20 78 – 13 = **Answer** ☐

Q21 4 x 5 = **Answer** ☐

Q22 Express 12.5% as a decimal **Answer** ☐

Q23 11 x 15 = **Answer** ☐

Q24 Convert 120% to a decimal **Answer** ☐

Q25 Multiply 600 by 30 **Answer** ☐

Q26 9 x 7 = **Answer** ☐

Q27 Express 1/5 as a percentage **Answer** ☐

Q28 3/10 of 30 = **Answer** ☐

Q29 How many grams make 1/5 of 1 kg? **Answer** ☐

Q30 47 + 35 = **Answer** ☐

Q31 1/4 and 8/32 are equivalent fractions (True or False) **Answer** ☐

Q32 4 x 6 = **Answer** ☐

Q33 210 – 66 = **Answer** [ ]

Q34 How many centimetres make 3/10 of 2 metres? **Answer** [ ]

Q35 76 + 22 = **Answer** [ ]

Q36 14 x 5 = **Answer** [ ]

Q37 2/5 of 200 = **Answer** [ ]

Q38 How many litres make up 1,500 cm^3? **Answer** [ ]

Q39 36 is a square number (True or False) **Answer** [ ]

Q40 20 x 19 = **Answer** [ ]

Q41 3 is a factor of 18 (True or False) **Answer** [ ]

Q42 7 x 12 = **Answer** [ ]

Q43 200 divided by 8 is **Answer** [ ]

Q44 How many feet and inches is 42 inches? **Answer** [ ]

Q45 147 – 98 = **Answer** [ ]

Q46 11 x 7 = **Answer** [ ]

Q47 15 + 27 = **Answer** [ ]

Q48 Express the decimal 0.8 as a fraction in its simplest form **Answer** [ ]

Q49 9 x 3 = **Answer** [ ]

Q50 34 – 21 = **Answer**

Q51 Divide 300 by the ratio 2:1 **Answer**

Q52 48 + 19 = **Answer**

Q53 Multiply 0.025 by ten thousand **Answer**

Q54 7 x 15 = **Answer**

Q55 18 – 11 = **Answer**

Q56 Divide 2,100 by 7 **Answer**

Q57 How many 125 gm portions can you get from 1 kg? **Answer**

Q58 9 x 9 = **Answer**

Q59 Which of the following is not a cubed number: 8, 27, 64, 94, 125? **Answer**

Q60 113 + 56 = **Answer**

End of test

Quick test 3

Again this test contains 60 questions and you are allowed only 10 seconds a question. So try to answer all the questions in 10 minutes.

Why not set yourself a challenge? Score quick test 2 and go over any questions that you got wrong. Now set out to beat your last quick test score. Then you can prove to yourself that you really are improving.

But before you take this next test, take some time to revise any operation that you are getting wrong, skipping or slow at. For example if you are slow at converting fractions to equivalents, revise this for a while, then take this test feeling confident that you will do better.

To beat your last score you really are going to have to take the test seriously. It is harder than the last test. So go over any questions you got wrong in test 2 and revise the principle behind the question. If you ran out of time before you could complete all the questions in test 2, revise your multiplication and division until you are quicker and more confident. As soon as you begin, push yourself along as hard as you can. Do not spend too long on any one question, and keep going to the very end.

Remember find a comfortable quiet place where you will not be interrupted, and use a stopwatch or the stopwatch function on a mobile phone to time yourself exactly.

You will need a pencil to write down the answers, but do not use a calculator.

Do not turn the page until you are ready to begin.

Q1 What is half of 36? **Answer** [ ]

Q2 What number do you get if you multiply 12 by 5 and then divide the answer by 10? **Answer** [ ]

Q3 3 x 5 = **Answer** [ ]

Q4 Which of the suggested answers has two numbers that are both whole number multiples of 4?

A 16, 18, 12 B 7, 11, 13 C 21, 22, 24 **Answer** [ ]

Q5 7 x 6 = **Answer** [ ]

Q6 Which of these numbers is a multiple of 6, 8 and 12?

36 32 48 30 52 **Answer** [ ]

Q7 How many days are there in January? **Answer** [ ]

Q8 What does the < symbol mean?

Greater than Less than Equal to **Answer** [ ]

Q9 What was the year seventeen years before 2001? **Answer** [ ]

Q10 3 x 6 = **Answer** [ ]

Q11 What is 4 cubed? **Answer** [ ]

Q12 At what temperature in degrees centigrade does water boil? **Answer** [ ]

Q13 What number do you get if you divide 18 by 6 and then multiply the answer by 4?

9 12 18

Answer ☐

Q14 $51 \div 3 =$ **Answer** ☐

Q15 What does the $\leq$ symbol mean?

Less than Greater than Equal to
Equal to or less than

Answer ☐

Q16 If it is 2 o'clock now what will the time be in 1 hour and 45 minutes? **Answer** ☐

Q17 What power of 2 makes 16? **Answer** ☐

Q18 Is 9 a whole number factor of 18? (Yes or No) **Answer** ☐

Q19 $19 + 11 + 8 =$ **Answer** ☐

Q20 How many grams are there in half a kilogram? **Answer** ☐

Q21 15 minutes is how many seconds? **Answer** ☐

Q22 If the time is twelve fifteen what will be the time in twenty minutes? **Answer** ☐

Q23 $73 - 16 =$ **Answer** ☐

Q24 $23 - 5 + 2 =$ **Answer** ☐

Q25 Is 18 a cubed number? (Yes or No) **Answer** ☐

Q26 What day of the week it is three days after Wednesday? **Answer** ☐

Q27 What number do you start with if you multiply it by 5 then double it and get the answer 100?

15 5 10

Answer ☐

Q28 80 centimetres is equal to how many millimetres?

Answer ☐

Q29 What does the > symbol mean?

Answer ☐

Q30 17 + 4 – 6 =

Answer ☐

Q31 Which one of the following numbers can you divide exactly with 6?

32 43 54

Answer ☐

Q32 What is half of one hour and 30 minutes?

Answer ☐

Q33 What number do you start with if you multiply it by 10, then divide it by 3 and then halve it to get the figure 20?

9 1 12

Answer ☐

Q34 3 – 4 + 7 =

Answer ☐

Q35 12 x 12 =

Answer ☐

Q36 9 x 3 =

Answer ☐

Q37 The reciprocal value of 8 =

0.1 0.04 0.125

Answer ☐

Q38 5 x 6 =

Answer ☐

Q39 Is 16 a square number? (Yes or No) **Answer** ☐

Q40 7 x 7 = **Answer** ☐

Q41 What is 3 raised to the power of 3? **Answer** ☐

Q42 11 x 4 = **Answer** ☐

Q43 Simplify the ratio 4:12 **Answer** ☐

Q44 If 2/9 is equivalent to 12/?, what is the value of the unknown denominator?

54 18 27 **Answer** ☐

Q45 52 x 4 = **Answer** ☐

Q46 The reciprocal value of 4 is:

0.5 0.25 0.2 **Answer** ☐

Q47 24 x 3 = **Answer** ☐

Q48 If a square has an area of $25m^2$ what is the length of its sides? **Answer** ☐

Q49 84 ÷ 2 = **Answer** ☐

Q50 Is the sequence of 3, 5, 7, 11, 13:
Even numbers Odd numbers
Prime numbers? **Answer** ☐

Q51 60 ÷ 5 = **Answer** ☐

Q52 Which of the suggested answers is a decimal approximation of π?

1.25 3.14 4.45

Answer

Q53 $48 \div 6 =$

Answer

Q54 Which has the highest value, 18 or 2^4?

Answer

Q55 $72 \div 12 =$

Answer

Q56 If $3x + 3 = 18$ what is the value of x?

Answer

Q57 If you divide 77 by 11 you get the number:

Answer

Q58 1, 2 and 4 are whole number factors of which number?

4 5 6

Answer

Q59 The reciprocal value of 5 is

Answer

Q60 Simplify the ratio 16 : 40

Answer

End of test

Quick test 4

This is another 60-question test for which you are allowed 10 minutes.

You should realize by now that if you do not know your multiplication tables you cannot possible do well in this type of test. The same goes for any test of your numerical reasoning. Do not risk attending for a real test unless you know your tables off by heart.

Take some time to revise them and then come back to try another quick test. Our minds are wonderful things, but can be lazy if we allow them to be. We can so easily convince ourselves that we know something when in fact we do not. The only way to tell is to test yourself and try to beat your last score. So take the test seriously. As soon as you begin, push yourself along as hard as you can. Do not spend too long on any one question, and keep going to the very end.

Remember find a comfortable quiet place where you will not be interrupted, and use a stopwatch or the stopwatch function on a mobile phone to time yourself exactly.

Again you will need a pencil to write down the answers. Scrap paper is useful too but do not use a calculator.

Do not turn the page until you are ready to begin.

Q1 $9 \times 12 = 108$ (True or False) **Answer** [ ]

Q2 $88 - 33 =$ **Answer** [ ]

Q3 $8 \times 6 = 47$ (True or False) **Answer** [ ]

Q4 $36 + 36 =$ **Answer** [ ]

Q5 $27 - 8 =$ **Answer** [ ]

Q6 $6 \times 15 = 75$ (True or False) **Answer** [ ]

Q7 $119 - 63 =$ **Answer** [ ]

Q8 $87 + 112 =$ **Answer** [ ]

Q9 $11 \times 6 =$ **Answer** [ ]

Q10 $336 - 172 = 164$ (True or False) **Answer** [ ]

Q11 $44 + 63 =$ **Answer** [ ]

Q12 $14 \times 3 =$ **Answer** [ ]

Q13 $211 + 198 = 409$ (True or False) **Answer** [ ]

Q14 $21 \times 5 =$ **Answer** [ ]

Q15 $139 - 21 = 119$ (True or False) **Answer** [ ]

Q16 Match 31,386 to how it is written in words:
A Thirty one thousand, three hundred and eighty six
B Three hundred and thirteen thousand, three hundred and eighty six
C Three hundred and thirteen thousand and eighty six **Answer** ☐

Q17 99 + 198 = **Answer** ☐

Q18 What is 500 MORE than 325? **Answer** ☐

Q19 9.9 + 2.1 = **Answer** ☐

Q20 What is 500 LESS than 1,463? **Answer** ☐

Q21 What number do you start with if you halve it, multiply it by 7 then divide it with 6 to get the figure 7?

7 12 9 **Answer** ☐

Q22 What is 500 MORE than 20,696?

20,196 21,196 **Answer** ☐

Q23 What number do you start with if you multiply it by 3 then divide it by 12 to get the figure 10? **Answer** ☐

Q24 What is 2,101 MORE than 56? **Answer** ☐

Q25 What number do you start with if you multiply it by itself and then multiply the answer by 4 to get 36? **Answer** ☐

Q26 What is 128 MORE than 976? **Answer** ☐

Q27 1005 + 991 = **Answer** ☐

Q28 What is 2,004 LESS than 10,003? **Answer** ☐

Q29 198 + 197 + 196 = **Answer** ☐

Q30 What is the highest place value in the number 105,302?
A Hundred thousands B Ten thousands
C Tenths D Hundredths **Answer** ☐

Q31 77 + 87 = **Answer** ☐

Q32 What is the lowest place value in the number 983.5?
A Hundreds B Ones
C Tenths D Hundredths **Answer** ☐

Q33 Which of the following divides exactly by 9?

64 54 74 84 **Answer** ☐

Q34 Match the sum to the answer. Sum: 100 ÷ 10
Answer: 1 10 100 **Answer** ☐

Q35 What is 20% of 30? **Answer** ☐

Q36 Divide 334 by 1000 **Answer** ☐

Q37 If you divide 40 by 5 and then multiply the answer by 3 what number do you get? **Answer** ☐

Q38 Divide 349 by 10000 **Answer** ☐

Q39 Which of the following numbers can be divided exactly with both 4 and 3?

12 15 16 32 36 48 **Answer** ☐

Q40 The fraction 3/4 is equivalent to what percentage? **Answer** ☐

Q41 What number do you start with if you multiply it by 3, then double it and get the answer 30? **Answer** ☐

Q42 What number do you get if you divide 84 by 7? **Answer** ☐

Q43 What is 7/12th of 60 minutes? **Answer** ☐

Q44 Divide 0.045 by 100 **Answer** ☐

Q45 Multiply 0.932 by 100 **Answer** ☐

Q46 What is the decimal equivalent of 4%? **Answer** ☐

Q47 Work out -3 + -3 = **Answer** ☐

Q48 Work out -2 – -2 = **Answer** ☐

Q49 Work out -1 + 9 = **Answer** ☐

Q50 Work out -7 – +5 = **Answer** ☐

Q51 Work out -6 + 6 = **Answer** ☐

Q52 Work out -14 – 3 = **Answer** ☐

Q53 Work out 10 – -8 = **Answer** ☐

Q54 What is 1/9 of 63 km? **Answer** ☐

Q55 What is 4/5ths of 50 minutes? **Answer** ☐

Q56 What is 2/5ths of 10 metres^2? **Answer** ☐

Q57 What equivalent fraction does 3/9ths cancel to? **Answer** ☐

Q58 What equivalent fraction does 8/12ths cancel to? **Answer** ☐

Q59 What equivalent fraction does 25/40 cancel to? **Answer** ☐

Q60 What is 1/6th of 3? **Answer** ☐

End of test

Quick test 5

This is another 60-question test for which you are allowed 10 minutes.

This one is a bit harder but it still tests essential skills. You might not be able to answer all the questions in the time allowed. But if you face a high-level test like for example the SHL graduate battery or the Civil Service fast-stream, you should be able to answer many of the questions in far less than 10 seconds, allowing you longer to spend on the more time-demanding questions.

I am not suggesting that you will find a question like 'What is the equivalent fraction to 12.5%?' in the SHL battery. The point I am making is that you will not do really well in the SHL battery and tests like it unless you can do sums like this really quickly.

Many of the questions in a numerical reasoning test at the graduate level break down to a series of these sorts of sums. If you are slower in these numeracy skills than other candidates, or if you make too many avoidable mistakes, you will not get a very good score. To do well at this level you need to be able to get these calculations right every time, and really fast.

If you find it almost impossible to do these questions this fast, don't give up because if you keep going with this sort of practice you will get much faster and more accurate. Practice and more practice is the key.

To complete the test you will have to work very quickly. Skip any question that you cannot answer straight away. But try not to miss out too many!

To get a good score you will have to be both well practised and confident.

Do not turn over the page until you are ready to begin.

Q1 Change 3/25 into a percentage **Answer** ☐

Q2 What is 3% of 50,000? **Answer** ☐

Q3 What number do you start with if you multiply it by 4, then double it and then divide it by 12 to get the figure 4?

6 7 8 **Answer** ☐

Q4 If 6/8 is equivalent to ?/32 what is the value of the unknown numerator? **Answer** ☐

Q5 What is 30 as a percentage of 200? **Answer** ☐

Q6 What is 8% of 60? **Answer** ☐

Q7 Which number is a multiple of 3, 4 and 6?

6 10 19 23 36 **Answer** ☐

Q8 Which is the smallest?

A 0.2 B 1/2 C 1/4 **Answer** ☐

Q9 What number do you start with if you halve it, then divide it by 4, then multiply it by 6 to get 12? **Answer** ☐

Q10 Which is the smallest?

2/8 0.25 1/5 **Answer** ☐

Q11 7 – -6 = **Answer** ☐

Q12 What is the smallest? 10% 1/6 0.33 **Answer** ☐

Q13 What is 1/3 of 24? **Answer** ☐

Q14 Which is the larger?

0.3 3/12 **Answer** ☐

Q15 Increase 400 by 40% **Answer** ☐

Q16 Which is the largest?

0.4 2/5 50% **Answer** ☐

Q17 18% of 600 is? **Answer** ☐

Q18 Change 0.44 into a percentage **Answer** ☐

Q19 Convert 80% into its equivalent fraction expressed in its simplest form **Answer** ☐

Q20 Change 0.01 into a percentage:

A 10% B 100% C 1% D 5% **Answer** ☐

Q21 2 – -9 = **Answer** ☐

Q22 Change 25% into a fraction **Answer** ☐

Q23 What number do you start with if you divide it by 4, halve it and then multiply it by 5 to get the figure 20? **Answer** ☐

Q24 Change 3/10 into a percentage **Answer** ☐

Q25 What distance is travelled in 2 minutes at 4 m/s? **Answer** ☐

Q26 Change 5/20 into a percentage — Answer ☐

Q27 Change 70% into a decimal — Answer ☐

Q28 Which is the larger?

63% 0.83 — Answer ☐

Q29 Change 45% into a decimal — Answer ☐

Q30 -4 – -10 = — Answer ☐

Q31 Which is the smaller?

12.5% 1/7 — Answer ☐

Q32 1.94 + 17.07 = — Answer ☐

Q33 What is the distance travelled at 50 km/h in 2.5 hours? — Answer ☐

Q34 Which number is closest to 1?

0.12 0.91 0.56 — Answer ☐

Q35 Which number is closest to 1?

1.08 1.11 0.80 1.41 — Answer ☐

Q36 How many times does 27 divide into 108? — Answer ☐

Q37 What is 30% of 1200? — Answer ☐

Q38 What number can you multiply by itself to get 900? — Answer ☐

Q39 What number can you add to itself to get 240? **Answer**

Q40 What number can you multiply by itself to get 81? **Answer**

Q41 1.64 + 13.6 = **Answer**

Q42 What number did you start with if you multiply it by itself and then multiply the answer by 5 to get 20?

A 1 B 2 C 3 D 4 **Answer**

Q43 3/4 of 1 kg is how many grams? **Answer**

Q44 Which two numbers are both multiples of 6?
9 8 11 14 36 20 24 **Answer**

Q45 50 + 40 + 90 + 10 = **Answer**

Q46 -2 – +9 = **Answer**

Q47 What number do you get if you divide 72 by 8? **Answer**

Q48 What number do you get if you divide 66 by 6? **Answer**

Q49 16.3 – 8.2 = **Answer**

Q50 7 + – 3 = **Answer**

Q51 20% of 24 km is more than 5 kilometres (True or False) **Answer**

Q52 - 4 – - 9 = **Answer** ☐

Q53 Which number can you divide exactly by 7?
93 81 77 **Answer** ☐

Q54 How many km are 5/6 of 30 km? **Answer** ☐

Q55 ? + 11.9 = 17 **Answer** ☐

Q56 Which number can you divide exactly with 8?
72 49 63 **Answer** ☐

Q57 How many ml are in 6/10 of a litre? **Answer** ☐

Q58 Which number can you divide exactly with both 6 and 9?

42 30 36 45 **Answer** ☐

Q59 -2 + -7 = **Answer** ☐

Q60 360.3 – 170.3 = **Answer** ☐

End of test

3

The secrets of number sequencing revealed

Sequencing

Each question comprises a series of numbers with one number in the series missing. It is your task to identify from the suggested answers which number completes the series. To do this you have to first work out the relationship between the given numbers.

This style of question was once very fashionable. Today they are less common in numeracy tests relating to employment, and are more likely to be found in IQ tests. They are, however, really well worth practising. Whether or not you face this type of test you should still work through this chapter. This type of question requires you to demonstrate a strong command of the key operations of maths, and to problem solve by trying a number of different possible solutions until you find one that fits. These are techniques that will serve you really well in all sorts of test of your numeracy skills. To help you develop these skills the first 40 questions have been placed under headings that broadly describe the relationship on which the question is based.

If you find this style of question a complete enigma, then take heart because you will find here lots of questions on which to practise. All you need to do is find the time to go through them. Make sure that you pause occasionally and review the explanations, then go back to more practice. It will not be long before you show a considerable improvement in your score.

Practise and you will soon find that you can get these questions right very quickly. It's great for your confidence.

Once again this chapter is a calculator free zone! Answers and explanations are provided from page 152.

The first 40 questions

There are eight very common relationships on which most number sequence questions are based. I have organized the first 40 questions in this chapter under broad headings which describe these eight relationships, and each heading is followed by five example questions. Use these to become familiar with the most common types of sequence question.

Add the same number

Example question:

Q1 2, 4, 6, 8, ? **Answer** 10

Explanation: at each step 2 is added.

Q2 18, 24, ?, 36, 42 **Answer**

Q3 ?, 66, 77, 88, 99 **Answer**

Q4 63, ?, 81, 90 **Answer**

Q5 70, ?, 84, 91 **Answer**

Subtract the same number

Worked example:

Q6	12, 10, 8, ?	**Answer**	6

Explanation: subtract 2 each step starting with 2 x 6 = 12.

Q7	54, 48, ?, 36	**Answer**	
Q8	49, ?, 35, 28	**Answer**	
Q9	27, 24, 21, ?	**Answer**	
Q10	132, 120, ?, 96	**Answer**	

Multiply or divide by the same number

Worked example:

Q11	4, 8, 16, ?	**Answer**	32

Explanation: the previous number is multiplied by 2 at each step.

Q12	3125, 625, ?, 25	**Answer**	
Q13	27, ?, 243, 729	**Answer**	
Q14	128, ?, 512, 1024	**Answer**	
Q15	1, 6, 36, ?, 1296	**Answer**	

Add a changing number

Worked example:

Q16 2, ?, 9, 14 **Answer** 5

Explanation: 3 is added at the first step to give 5, then 4 is added to give 9, then 5 to give 14.

Q17 ?, 20, 25, 31 **Answer**

Q18 30, 31, 33, ? **Answer**

Q19 17, ?, 28, 35 **Answer**

Q20 100, 150, ?, 253 **Answer**

Subtract a changing number

Worked example:

Q21 45, ?, 34, 30 **Answer** 39

Explanation: 45 (– 6), 39 (– 5), 34 (– 4), 30.

Q22 9, 6, ?, 3 **Answer**

Q23 ?, 20, 12, 3 **Answer**

Q24 99, 84, 70, ? **Answer**

Q25 ?, 18, 16, 15 **Answer**

A sequence of multiples

Worked example:

Q26 100, ?, 115, 130, 150 **Answer** 105

Explanation: 100(+ 5x1), 105 (+ 5x2), 115 (+ 5x3), 130 (+ 5x4), 150.

Q27 7, 13, ?, 31, 43 **Answer**

Q28 ?, 24, 36, 52, 72 **Answer**

Q29 7, 10, 16, ?, 37 **Answer**

Q30 10, ?, 40, 70, 110 **Answer**

A sequence of multiples in reverse

Worked example

Q31 102, 90, 72, ?, 18 **Answer** 48

Explanation: 102 (– 6x2=12), 90(– 6x3=18), 72 (– 6x4=24), 48 (– 6x5=30), 18.

Q32 68, ?, 50, 38, 24 **Answer**

Q33 42, ?, 30, 18, 2 **Answer**

Q34 140, 120, ?, 50, 0 **Answer**

Q35 131, ?, 86, 59, 29 **Answer**

Sequences that test your knowledge of factors, powers and prime numbers

Worked example:

Q36 2, 3, 5, ? Answer 7

Explanation: these are the first four numbers in the series of prime numbers: numbers that only have two whole-number factors, 1 and themselves. For example, 2 is divisible only by the whole numbers 1 and 2. It is also the only even prime number.

Q37 1, 8, ?, 64 Answer

Q38 1, 2, ?, 6 Answer

Q39 9, 27, ?, 243, 729 Answer

Q40 ?, 125, 625, 3125 Answer

160 more number sequence questions

These questions are based on the same eight relationships as the first 40 sequence questions, only these are mixed up and there are no clues as to the type of question like those given by the broad headings above. You must first identify which type of sequence question you face, then complete the sequence to answer the question. The fact that there are so many questions means that you can develop endurance and concentration, which are also necessary skills if you are to do well in a test.

If you prefer, take 40 of these questions and attempt them against the clock. Use the same suggested time as the sequencing test in Chapter 6. If you find that you cannot complete these questions quickly enough, you will need to go back to revise more of your maths. You will find that you can only get these questions right quickly when you have a high command of the key operations, and the confidence to try one solution, and when it does not work, try another.

Develop a good test technique by not spending too long on any one question. If you hit a number of questions you find hard, don't give up: you might soon come to a section of questions in which you can excel.

Remember this: doing well in a test is a matter not simply of intelligence, but also of hard work, determination and systemic preparation.

Q41 1, 6, 11, 16, ? **Answer** ☐

Q42 1, 2, 3, 5, 6, 10, ?, 30 **Answer** ☐

Q43 198, 144, ?, 63, 36, 18 **Answer** ☐

Q44 ?, 28, 35, 42 **Answer** ☐

Q45 ?, 50, 41, 33 **Answer** ☐

Q46 50, ?, 155, 218, 288 **Answer** ☐

Q47 10, 13, 16, 19, ? **Answer** ☐

Q48 ?, 2, 4, 8 **Answer** ☐

Q49. 1, ?, 9, 16, 25 **Answer** ☐

Q50 99, 90, 81, ? **Answer** ☐

Q51 ?, 16, 32, 64 **Answer** ☐

Q52 11, 22, 34, ? **Answer** ☐

Q53 110, 122, 134, 146, ? **Answer** ☐

Q54 70, 102, ?, 178, 222 **Answer** ☐

Q55 30, 65, ?, 150, 200, **Answer** ☐

Q56 32, 64, ?, 256 Answer

Q57 32, ?, 104, 152, 208 Answer

Q58 33, 24, ?, 3 Answer

Q59 4, 12, ?, 108 Answer

Q60 40, 61, 85, ?, 142 Answer

Q61 ?, 17, 19, 23, 29 Answer

Q62 66, 84, ?, 138, 174 Answer

Q63 200, 130, 59, ? Answer

Q64 25, 61, 109, ?, 241 Answer

Q65 ?, 20, 40, 80, 160 Answer

Q66 ?, 3, 9, 27 Answer

Q67 ?, 40, 35, 30 Answer

Q68 ?, 91, 171, 261 Answer

Q69 9, ?, 729, 6561 Answer

Q70 24, ?, 68, 96, 128 Answer

Q71 10, 100, 1,000, 10,000, ? Answer

Q72 36, 48, ?, 72 Answer

Q73 22, 43, 71, ?, 148 Answer

Q74 120, ?, 77, 54 Answer

Q75 ?, 35, 46, 58 Answer

Q76 ?, 67, 81, 102, 130 Answer

Q77 1, 2, ?, 8, 16 Answer

Q78 54, ?, 42, 36 Answer

Q79 1, ?, 25, 125 Answer

Q80 75, ?, 78, 81 Answer

Q81 3, 1, ?, 0 Answer

Q82 12, ?, 18, 21 Answer

Q83 400, 200, ?, 50, 25 Answer

Q84 48, 36, ?, 12 Answer

Q85 1, ?, 49, 343 Answer

Q86 71, 88, ?, 125 Answer

Q87 120, ?, 93, 66, 30 Answer

Q88 50, 55, ?, 65 Answer

Q89 24, ?, 36, 42, 48 Answer

Q90 89, 70, ?, 35 Answer

Q91 ?, 60, 48, 30, 6 Answer

Q92 1, 2, ?, 22 Answer

Q93 101, 1010, ?, 101000 Answer

Q94 ?, 120, 131, 143 Answer

Q95 ?, 10, 3, -4 Answer

Q96 ?, 54, 34, 12 Answer

Q97 1, 2, ?, 4, 6, 12 Answer

Q98 108, 99, ?, 81 Answer

Q99 0.25, 1, ?, 16 Answer

Q100 13, ?, 32, 43 Answer

Q101 120, 80, 40, 0, ? Answer

Q102 137, ?, 88, 62 Answer

Q103 5, 7, ?, 13 Answer

Q104 ?, 200, 116, 44, -16 Answer

Q105 8, 16, 25, ? Answer

Q106 28, 21, 14, ? Answer

Q107 ?, 54, 63, 72 **Answer** ☐

Q108 90, 75, ?, 45 **Answer** ☐

Q109 108, 97, 75, ?, -2 **Answer** ☐

Q110 60, ?, 84, 96, 108 **Answer** ☐

Q111 312, ?, 223, 177 **Answer** ☐

Q112 132, ?, 96, 60, 12 **Answer** ☐

Q113 27, 30, ?, 36 **Answer** ☐

Q114 Which suggested answer correctly identifies the following sequence: 1, 8, 27, 64, 125

A The sequence of squared numbers ☐

B The sequence of cubed numbers ☐

C The sequence of prime numbers? ☐

Q115 Which suggested answer correctly identifies the following sequence: 2, 3, 5, 7, 11, 13, 17

A The sequence of squared numbers ☐

B The sequence of cubed numbers ☐

C The sequence of prime numbers? ☐

Q116 Which suggested answer correctly identifies the following sequence: 1, 4, 9, 16, 25

A The sequence of squared numbers ☐

B The sequence of cubed numbers ☐

C The sequence of prime numbers? ☐

Q117 123, 83, 42, ? Answer

Q118 61, 31, 11, ? Answer

Q119 7, ?, 343, 2401 Answer

Q120 ?, 33, 30, 27 Answer

Q121 243, 81, 27, ? Answer

Q122 8, 26, 45, ? Answer

Q123 16, ?, 49, 67 Answer

Q124 1, 2, 3, 4, 6, ?, 12, 18, 36 Answer

Q125 78, 63, ?, 36 Answer

Q126 93, 81, 65, ?, 21 Answer

Q127 72, 66, ?, 54 Answer

Q128 21, 27, ?, 42 Answer

Q129 24, 32, 40, ? Answer

Q130 ?, 25, 18, 10 Answer

Q131 100, ?, 93, 79, 58, 30 Answer

Q132 27, ?, 125, 216 Answer

Q133 ?, 38, 29, 19 Answer

Q134 80, 88, ?, 128, 160 Answer

Q135 7, 26, 46, ? Answer

Q136 30, 52, 85, ?, 184 Answer

Q137 36, 49, 64, ? Answer

Q138 ?, 84, 88, 93 Answer

Q139 2, ?, 65, 110, 164 Answer

Q140 330, ?, 191, 123 Answer

Q141 194, 144, 104, 74, ? Answer

Q142 ?, 56, 80, 116, 164 Answer

Q143 3, 33, ?, 96 Answer

Q144 30, 24, ?, 12 Answer

Q145 54, ?, 124, 174, 234 Answer

Q146 1, ?, 7, 14 Answer

Q147 6, 21, 37, ? Answer

Q148 ?, 92, 110, 134, 164 Answer

Q149 ?, 30, 27, 24 Answer

Q150 19, 33, 49, ?, 87 Answer

Q151 1, 2, ?, 8, 16 Answer

Q152 ?, 16, 14, 13 Answer

Q153 ?, 22, 46, 82, 130 Answer

Q154 36, 45, ?, 63 Answer

Q155 60, 71, ?, 96 Answer

Q156 28, 32, ?, 40 Answer

Q157 ?, 22, 28, 37, 49 Answer

Q158 ?, 64, 512, 4096 Answer

Q159 ?, 120, 175, 235, 300 Answer

Q160 20, ?, 17, 17 Answer

Q161 41, ?, 82, 104 Answer

Q162 10, ?, 0.1, 0.01 Answer

Q163 80, 72, 64, ? Answer

Q164 1, 2, 3, 6, ?, 18 Answer

Q165 54, ?, 234, 342, 462 Answer

Q166 ?, 123, 127, 132 Answer

Q167 8, ?, 122, 188, 260 Answer

Q168 16, 25, ?, 49 Answer

Q169 21, 28, ?, 45 Answer

Q170 54, 45, ?, 27 Answer

Q171 ?, 37, 43, 51, 61 Answer

Q172 64, ?, 216, 343 Answer

Q173 55, 38, ?, 7 Answer

Q174 72, 104, 144, ?, 248 Answer

Q175 48, 32, 17, ? Answer

Q176 88, 96, ?, 112 Answer

Q177 1, 3, ?, 27 Answer

Q178 102, 72, ?, 42, 42 Answer

Q179 ?, 80, 48, 12 Answer

Q180 110, ?, 132, 143 Answer

Q181 216, 176, 144, ?, 104 Answer

Q182 74, 55, 37, ? Answer

Q183 1, 2 , 4, 8, ?, 32 Answer

Q184 36, ?, 24, 18 Answer

Q185 7776, 1296, ?, 36 **Answer** [ ]

Q186 43, ?, 78, 97 **Answer** [ ]

Q187 ?, 18, 27, 36 **Answer** [ ]

Q188 120, ?, 35, -15, -70 **Answer** [ ]

Q189 ?, 65, 70, 75 **Answer** [ ]

Q190 27, 22, ?, 9 **Answer** [ ]

Q191 288, 211, ?, 90, 46 **Answer** [ ]

Q192 44, 48, ?, 56 **Answer** [ ]

Q193 ?, 54, 29, 5 **Answer** [ ]

Q194 1, 2, 4, 5, 10, ? **Answer** [ ]

Q195 77, ?, 50, 32 **Answer** [ ]

Q196 ?, 129, 160, 192 **Answer** [ ]

Q197 84, 72, ?, 48 **Answer** [ ]

Q198 512, 256, ?, 64 **Answer** [ ]

Q199 5,000, 200, ?, 0.32 **Answer** [ ]

Q200 30, 42, ?, 69, 84 **Answer** [ ]

End of test

4

Become brilliant at number problems

This chapter comprises 100 questions of a type commonly found in numeracy tests. So many questions means that you can undertake hours of practice and witness some significant gains in your numeracy skills, confidence, speed and accuracy.

These questions require you to read a short passage describing a situation, then to undertake a calculation and record your answer in the answer box or identify it from a suggested list. Usually the maths in these questions is relatively straightforward. You are unlikely to be allowed to use a calculator, so the calculations can be worked out conveniently by hand. You are very unlikely to be expected to do an awkward long multiplication or division. Typically these questions test your command of addition, subtraction, multiplication, division, fractions, decimals, percentages, and quantities such as time, distance and value. You will have revised these operations in the previous chapters, and this practice will serve you well when attempting these questions.

There remains however, perhaps the greatest challenge with these questions: realizing correctly what the question requires of you. Many candidates find it hard to decide what calculation they must complete. The test author, of course, tries to make things worse by setting traps and tricking you into undertaking the wrong calculation. To help you to overcome this common difficultly I have organized some of the questions under headings that describe the task being examined, and in many of the explanations I describe what the question requires of you along with a working of the answer.

With practice you will become more confident and learn to quickly identify the correct calculation for these common questions. The extra practice will also ensure you continue to gain speed, accuracy and confidence in the essential mathematical operations. In Chapter 6 you will be able to put your new-found confidence into practice and take a realistic test of this style of question against the clock, and without the assistance of these broad headings.

No time limit is imposed in this chapter, but remember not to use a calculator. Answers and explanations are provided from page 101.

Further practice of this type of question is available from the following titles in the Kogan Page testing series: *How to Pass Numeracy Tests*, second edition, by Harry Tolley and Ken Thomas; *How to Pass Selection Tests*, third edition, by Mike Bryon and Sanjay Modha; *The Ultimate Psychometric Test Book* by Mike Bryon, and *How to Pass Graduate Psychometric Tests* by Mike Bryon.

Forty questions that do *not* involve percentages but may require you to work fractions and ratios

Q1 If 40 gadgets cost $1,000 or 90 cost $1,800, how much do you save on each gadget if you buy the bigger quantity?

Answer [ ]

Q2 If 3 containers each hold 20 litres and another 4 containers each hold 15 litres, what is the total capacity of all 7 containers?

Answer [ ]

Q3 If on average 13 complaints are received each day how many would you expect to receive over a 30-day period? **Answer** ☐

Q4 From a total of 13,700 processed applications for a credit card how many are declined if 10,290 cards are issued? **Answer** ☐

Q5 If 1 out of every 9 respondents in a survey answered positively, how many out of the total 225 respondents gave a negative answer? **Answer** ☐

Q6 How many boxes do you need if you have to pack 36 pairs of shoes into boxes that each hold 18 shoes? **Answer** ☐

Q7 If 17 households were found to produce 85 bottles for recycling, how many bottles would you expect 200 households to produce? **Answer** ☐

Q8 A team of 250 workers attend a health and safety briefing which lasts 30 minutes. How many hours of productive work are lost ? **Answer** ☐

Q9 If 50 calls are made each hour and of these 3 result in a sale, how many hours would it take to achieve 57 sales? **Answer** ☐

Q10 Over a five-day period 600 people visited an attraction. 1/3 attended on day one and 5/12 attended on day two. How many attendees visited the attraction over the last three days? **Answer** ☐

Q11 If 270 passengers have a combined hand luggage allowance of 4050 kg how much is the hand luggage allowance for each passenger? **Answer** [ ]

Q12 If the Azores are a group of islands 1,100 nautical miles from Lisbon, Portugal, and they are 4/9 of the way between Lisbon and Newfoundland, America, how far is it from Lisbon to Newfoundland? **Answer** [ ]

Q13 If a box contains 30 pairs of shoes how many shoes would 7 boxes contain? **Answer** [ ]

Q14 If a canteen can sit 57 people how many sittings are required to feed 228 people? **Answer** [ ]

Q15 If 6 eggs weigh 270 g how much would 4 eggs weigh? **Answer** [ ]

Q16 A cinema has 720 seats. If it is 5/6 full how many seats are unoccupied? **Answer** [ ]

Q17 If a population of 20,000 people kept 400 cats how many more cats would be needed to achieve a ratio of 1 cat to 40 people? **Answer** [ ]

Q18 If a bus is timetabled to arrive at a very busy terminal every 45 seconds how many should arrive in one hour? **Answer** [ ]

Q19 If a worker spends 7 hours a day in the office and 1/5 of this time is spent on the internet, how much time does this person spend on other activities? **Answer** [ ]

Q20 If 1/3 of a workforce of 765 are women, how many are men?

Answer [ ]

Q21 If a family with young children uses on average 21 bottles of milk a week, while a family with older children uses 14 bottles, how many more bottles of milk does a family with young children use in a year?

Answer [ ]

Q22 If 150 people are to attend a conference and a bus is available to transport them to the venue, what will be the minimum number of bus trips needed to transfer all the delegates if each bus has a capacity of 21?

Answer [ ]

Q23 If 1 in 3 people who live in a town with a population of 54,000 are aged over 60 years, how many people of this age group live in the town?

Answer [ ]

Q24 If a company manufactures T-shirts in the colours red, blue and white in the ratio 1:3:5, and it makes a total of 4050 T-shirts, how many are blue?

Answer [ ]

Q25 If for every ice-cream sold a busy café sells 6 cans of drink, and in one day 288 cans of drink are sold, how many ice creams did it sell that day?

Answer [ ]

Q26 If 600 people responded to a survey and 210 responded positively while 350 responded negatively, what is the ratio between positive and negative responses? (Express the ratio in its simplest form.)

Answer [ ]

Q27 At a sports venue a 3-day series attracted the following numbers of spectators: 34,640, 19,750 and 21,610. How many people attended in total? **Answer** ☐

Q28 To reach target a sales team must achieve on average 150 sales a month. At the end of the third quarter 1,200 sales have been achieved. How many sales must they realize during the last quarter to reach target? **Answer** ☐

Q29 If an item weighs 3.5 kg how much would 12 of these items weigh? **Answer** ☐

Q30 If an internet site receives an average of 90 hits an hour, how many hits would you expect in a week? **Answer** ☐

Q31 If 3,000 schoolchildren are served by 12 schools, by how many would the average number of children per school decrease if the authority was to open 3 more schools? **Answer** ☐

Q32 If 17,500 people attended a sporting fixture and 4/7 supported the winning side, how many present watched their team lose? **Answer** ☐

Q33 If a ferry service can carry a maximum of 2,000 passengers per sailing and it is on average 3/5 full during the summer but 3/8 full during the winter, how many fewer passengers are carried during a winter than summer sailing? **Answer** ☐

Q34 If a machine can produce 180 items per hour, how many could 2 machines produce in 25 minutes?

Answer ☐

Q35 How many illustrated pages does a 156-page book contain if the ratio between illustrated and non-illustrated pages is 4:9?

Answer ☐

Q36 If you tear a large sheet of paper into 9 pieces and then tear each of these pieces into 9 more, how many pieces of paper would there be?

Answer ☐

Q37 If 70 out of 520 guests at a hotel were children and 4/5 of the adult guests were men, how many women stayed at the hotel?

Answer ☐

Q38 If a bag contains 1 kg of sugar, 1.5 kg of coffee, 0.75 kg of tea, 0.5 kg of biscuits and a 1 kg slab of cake, how much do the combined contents weigh?

Answer ☐

Q39 If a van can hold 30 boxes and in each box there are 230 shoes, how many pairs does a fully loaded van contain?

Answer ☐

Q40 If a machine produces 115 parts a minute, how many parts would 3 machines produce in 15 minutes?

Answer ☐

Introducing percentage number problems

Eighteen number problem questions that introduce the common types of percentage calculation

Percentages of quantities

Worked example:

Q41 If a race occurs over 15 km and 25% of the distance remains, how many kilometres have the runners covered?

Answer 11.25 km or 11,250 m

Explanation: convert the percentage into a decimal (divide by 100) and multiply by the quantity. Take care to convert the quantities into the appropriate units as necessary. In this instance you are required to calculate not 25% of the distance (that is the distance that remains) but 75%, the distance covered. Divide 75 by 100 = 0.75 x 15 = 11.25 km.

Q42 If a journey normally takes 4 hours but a delay has increased this time by 20%, how long will this journey now take? (Express your answer in hours and minutes.)

Answer

Q43 If a 300g jar of coffee contains 15% more than the normal size, how much extra coffee do you get?

Answer

Percentage decrease

Worked example:

Q44 If a currency is devalued from $100 to $97, what is this decrease expressed as a percentage?

Answer 3%

Explanation: to calculate a percentage decrease, divide the amount of decrease by the original amount and multiply the answer by 100. In this example you have to find the percentage decrease from 100 to 97, so 100 - 97 = 3, 3 ÷ 100 = 0.03 x 100 = 3.

Q45 If a credit rating dropped from 1,000 (100%) to 250, what would this adjustment amount to as a percentage?

Answer

Q46 If the net profit on a highly successful line was to drop from 10% to 8.2%, what would this drop be, expressed as a percentage of the original net profit?

Answer

Percentage increase

Worked example:

Q47 If the number of insurance claims per 1,000 policies was to increase from 20 to 30, what is the percentage increase in claims?

Answer 50%

Explanation: calculate the percentage increase, then divide the increase by the original amount and multiply the answer by 100. In this instance the increase = 10 ÷ 20 (the original sum) = 0.5 x 100 = 50%.

Q48 If unit sales were to improve from 700 to 910 units, what is the improvement expressed as a percentage? **Answer** [ ]

Q49 If the items held in stock were to increase from 40 to 56, what would this increase be as a percentage? **Answer** [ ]

Percentage change

Worked example:

Q50 If the list price of a commodity is adjusted by 0.3 to a new high value of 2.8, what is the percentage change in value?

Answer 12% increase

Explanation: the adjustment leads to a new high, so this means the change is an increase. We can calculate the previous price was 2.8 – 0.3 = 2.5. We now must calculate the percentage change between 2.5 and 2.8. 2.5 – 2.8 = 0.3, 0.3 ÷ 2.5 = 0.12 x 100 = 12.

Q51 If the price of a commodity was adjusted by 0.35 downwards from 7.00, what is the percentage change in its value? **Answer** [ ]

Q52 If the list price of a commodity was adjusted up 21.6 from 36, what is the percentage change in its value? **Answer** [ ]

One number expressed as a percentage of another

Worked example:

Q53 50 people responded to a survey and 30 indicated that they had a passport. What percentage of the respondents said they held this document?

Answer | 60% increase |

Explanation: a percentage is a fraction with a denominator of 100. To express one number as a percentage of another, express the number as a fraction and then convert to an equivalent with a denominator of 100. In this instance you must convert 30/50 into an equivalent fraction, ?/100. Do this by multiplying top and bottom by 2 = 60/100 = 60%.

Q54 Four blood test results were positive out of a total of 16 samples tested; what percentage of the sample was positive?

Answer | |

Q55 If 1 in 5 cars are automatics what percentage of cars have this type of transmission?

Answer | |

Percentage profit and loss (of buying at cost price)

Worked example:

Q56 If you buy some high-yield stock at \$10 and sell it at \$14, what is the percentage profit or loss?

Answer | 40% profit |

Explanation: to find the percentage profit divide the amount of profit by the buying price and multiply by 100. To find the percentage loss divide the loss by the buying price and multiply by 100. In this instance 14 – 10 = 4, so profit = 4, 4 ÷ 10 = 0.4 x 100 = 40%. Do not forget to say whether it is a profit or a loss.

NOTE: Use this method to calculate all the profit and loss questions in this volume.

Q57 Panic selling led to a change in price from \$10 to \$8. What would the percentage loss be for anyone unfortunate to have bought and sold at these prices? **Answer**

Q58 In a rally the price of stock increased from \$60 to \$75. If you had bought at the lower price and sold at the higher price, what would be your percentage profit? **Answer**

Forty-two more number problems

Q59 16 people were asked if they had enjoyed their holiday. Four said they had not. What percentage of the respondents is this group? **Answer**

Q60 If it rained on two days out of a five-day period what was the percentage of days with rain? **Answer**

Q61 In the first quarter only 12 units were sold against a target of 80; what percentage of the target was realized? **Answer**

Q62 If the list price of an item is dropped by 4.4 from a price of 220.0, what is the percentage change in value? **Answer**

Q63 How many times larger is 530,000 than 5.3? **Answer**

Q64 A third of 72 eggs were brown but 3 of the brown ones were broken. What percentage of brown eggs were broken? **Answer**

Q65 If an 80 g bag of crisps contains 0.2 g of salt, what percentage of the 80 g is salt? **Answer** [ ]

Q66 If a new process meant that the same product could be made in 36 seconds instead of the previous 60 seconds, what is the saving in time as a percentage of the original production time? **Answer** [ ]

Q67 If you start a journey at 10.21 and stop for a one-hour break then resume the journey to arrive at 14.40, how many hours and minutes will you be travelling for? **Answer** [ ]

Q68 A telesales team of 12 are expected to make 2,400 calls a day. In fact they manage 2,640 calls each day for a whole week. What is the percentage change between the daily target number of calls and the actual number achieved? **Answer** [ ]

Q69 If you cycle at 18 km/hr how far can you travel in 40 minutes? **Answer** [ ]

Q70 If a gross return of $750 was made on an investment purchased at $2,500 what was the percentage of gross profit? **Answer** [ ]

Q71 If a car is sold at 8% less than its list price of $15,000, how much is it sold for? **Answer** [ ]

Q72 If the unit price of an item increased to 3.3 from 3, what is the new price expressed as a percentage of the original? **Answer** [ ]

Q73 If a farmer produces 2.5 tonnes less than the previous year's 12.5 tonnes of his crop, what was this year's crop as a percentage of the previous year's? **Answer**

Q74 What is the percentage increase between 45 and 48 minutes past an hour? **Answer**

Q75 If an item was bought for $12 and sold for $2.4 what would be the percentage loss? **Answer**

Q76 In a survey of 50 company secretaries 10 did not respond to a question regarding heath and safety and 6 responded negatively. What percentage of respondents of those responding answered negatively? **Answer**

Q77 If two shareholders respectively hold 1/8 and 1/4 of a company's shares, how many more must they obtain to realize a controlling interest of 51% of the total 48,000 shares? **Answer**

Q78 If 6/15 of a project was completed after 3 months and a further 3/5 was completed after 5 months, how much of the project remains? **Answer**

Q79 Against costs of $500 an income of $62.5 was recorded; what is this expressed as a percentage? **Answer**

Q80 If a litre of a liquid product is made by mixing 3 liquids in the ratio of 4: 2: 1 and you need 35 litres of the product, how many litres of the first ingredient do you need? **Answer**

Q81 5, 700 letters out of 6,000 were delivered on time; what percentage of the letters arrived late? **Answer** [ ]

Q82 If an asset with a book value of $650 was sold for $611 what was the percentage loss? **Answer** [ ]

Q83 A journey was expected to take 3 hours but it in fact took 1/5 longer; how long was the journey? **Answer** [ ]

Q84 The Very Cool Corporation reported a $15,000 improvement on the previous year's profit margin of 22%. Both years saw a turnover of $500,000. What was the percentage profit for the current year? **Answer** [ ]

Q85 If the reading on a scientific instrument increased from 0.5 to 0.7, what would this be expressed as a percentage increase? **Answer** [ ]

Q86 If a stock was to drop in value from $70 to $49 what would this change be expressed as a percentage? **Answer** [ ]

Q87 If the emergency services were able to improve their response time by 3%, how much quicker would they arrive at an incident that previously had a response time of 5 minutes? **Answer** [ ]

Q88 On a scale of 5 an independent test rated a new product at a disappointing 1.5; what is the percentage equivalent of this rating? **Answer** [ ]

Q89 If a workforce of 3,200 was restructured and 1 in 8 staff were made redundant during the first stage of the restructuring and a further 3/16 were sacked at stage 2, how many staff remained in the organization? **Answer**

Q90 If the working week was reduced from 40 hours to 32 hours what would be the percentage change? **Answer**

Q91 If bad debt means that only $7,000 was receivable against costs of $28,000, what would be the percentage loss? **Answer**

Q92 How many trucks would be needed to transport one million items, if each truck could carry 100 boxes, each box contains 10 packs and each pack contains 100 items? **Answer**

Q93 If a product generates a profit of $36,000 with operating costs of $204,000, what is the profit expressed as a percentage of total revenue? **Answer**

Q94 If the income generated is $12,000 and the operating costs are $9,360 what is the percentage profit? **Answer**

Q95 All but 13 seats were taken on a busy train service made up of 8 carriages each with 72 seats. If 40 people were standing how many passengers were on the service? **Answer**

Q96 In its distribution subsidiary the Diverse Group made a loss of $3,000 on a turnover of $150,000 but in its retail chain it showed a profit of $15,000 on a turnover of $850,000. What was the group's overall percentage profit or loss? **Answer** ☐

Q97 If two containers A and B hold a combined weight of 22 kg and 15.4 kg of this total is held by the larger container A, what percentage of the whole is held by container B? **Answer** ☐

Q98 If a company makes provision for 2% of its turnover to become bad debt but in one year it suffers 4.5% bad debt against a turnover of $600,000, how much more in $ of bad debt did the company suffer that year? **Answer** ☐

Q99 How long does a journey take if it begins at 13.25 and ends at 20.07? **Answer** ☐

Q100 If two products generated $6,000 profit on combined turnover of $120,000, and product A accounted for 1/2 of that profit and 1/10 of that turnover, what was the profit made on product A expressed as a percentage of the turnover made on that product? **Answer** ☐

5

Succeed in data interpretation tests

A hundred practice questions

This type of question is fast becoming the most common sort you are likely to come across in tests of your numeracy skills. It provides a table, chart or graph, and you have to interpret the information to answer a series of questions that follow. These questions will test all the numeracy skills that you have been practising in the preceding chapters. In addition, you need to be confident and well practised in the interpretation of data presented graphically.

Use the following 100 practice questions to further improve your command of the key numerical operations, and to acquire a confident effective approach to the interpretation of graphically presented numerical information. This practice will also help you to become more familiar with the subject matter of these questions (which are often drawn from business), the format in which information is presented and the vocabulary used.

Remember not to use a calculator. No time limit is imposed on these questions but in Chapter 6 you will find a timed 40-question practice test of data interpretation. Answers and explanations are provided from page 188.

You will find more practice questions and alternative explanations at the intermediate level in the following titles from the Kogan Page testing series: *How to Pass Numeracy Tests* by Harry Tolley and Ken Thomas, and *How to Pass Numeracy Reasoning Tests: A step by step guide to learning the basics* by Heidi Smith. If you feel you are now ready for more advanced questions of this type, they are available in the Kogan Page titles *How to Pass Advanced Numeracy Tests* and *How to Pass Graduate Psychometric Tests*, both by Mike Bryon.

Now for the questions!

Complete the table and then calculate each angle in the segment of the pie chart

Product	1	2	3	4	Total
Quantity	?	15	25	20	90
Angle	?	?	?	?	360

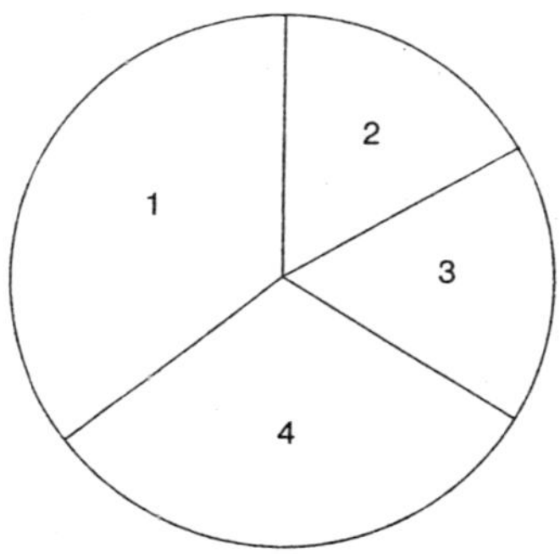

Q1 What is the quantity of product 1? **Answer** [ ]

Q2 Calculate the angle for segment 1. **Answer** [ ]

Q3 Calculate the angle for segment 2. **Answer** [ ]

Q4 Calculate the angle for segment 3. **Answer** ☐

Q5 Calculate the angle for segment 4. **Answer** ☐

Employment by industry

All figures given in millions

Year	2000	2005
All employment	22	24
Service industries	7.7	9.6
Manufacturing	1.98	2.64

Q6 In 2005 how many people were employed in manufacturing and service industries combined? **Answer** ☐

Q7 In 2005 what was manufacturing's share of all employment? **Answer** ☐

Q8 In 2000 what was the service industries' percentage share of all employment? **Answer** ☐

Q9 In 2000 what percentage of all employment was outside the service and manufacturing industries? **Answer** ☐

Q10 Between 2000 and 2005 did other sectors of employment (ie not service industries or manufacturing) increase or decrease their share of all employment?

Increase ☐ Decrease ☐ Cannot tell ☐

Sale volumes of old and new design

Below the same information is presented three ways. Compare the different formats to answer the questions.

Month	1	2	3	4
Old Design	1,500	1,000	500	250
New Design	1,000	?	?	1,250

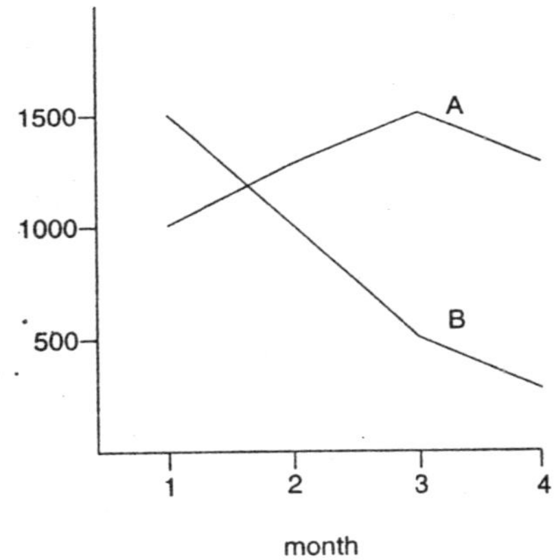

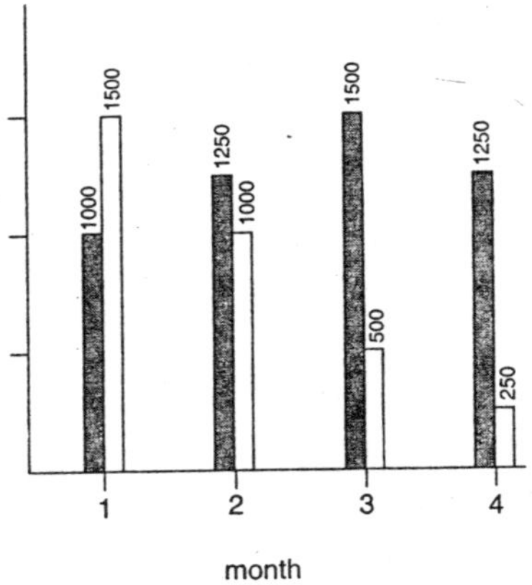

Q11 Which line on the line graph represents the old design?

A ☐ B ☐ Cannot tell ☐

Q12 What bar on the bar chart represents month 3 sales for the new design?

The shaded bar ☐ The unshaded bar ☐ Cannot tell ☐

Q13 For month 2 what is the value of sales for the new design? **Answer** ☐

Q14 Would the axis for the bar chart representing the monthly periods usually be labelled the x or y axis? **Answer** ☐

Sales by region from table to pie graph

Region	Sales
1	250
2	500
3	?
4	125
Total sales	1,500

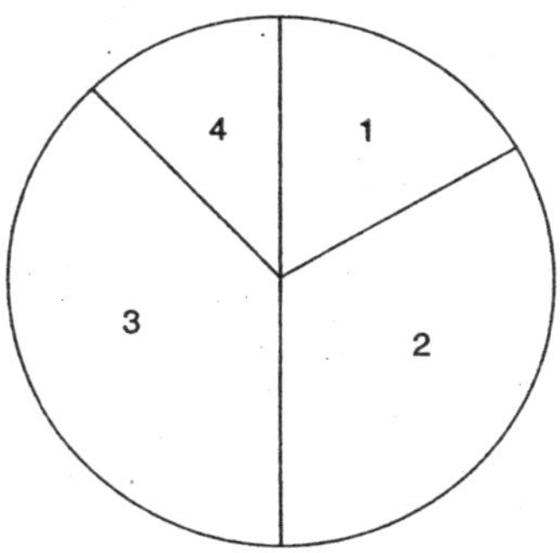

Q15 What region has the highest sales? **Answer** ☐

Q16 Calculate the angle for segment 1 of the pie graph. **Answer** ☐

Q17 What percentage of the total sales does Region 2 enjoy?

30% ☐ 33% ☐ 35% ☐ 40% ☐

Q18 Calculate the angle for segment 2. **Answer** ☐

Q19 Calculate the sales of Region 4 as a fraction of total sales. (Express the fraction in its simplest form.) **Answer** ☐

Q20 Calculate the angle for segment 3. **Answer** ☐

Analysis of a workforce by grade and gender

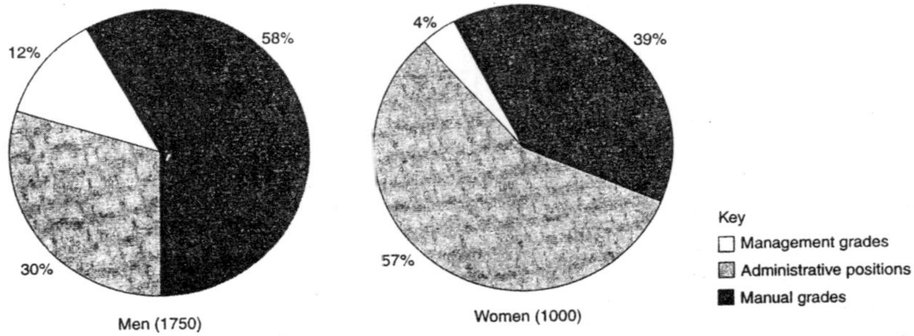

Q21 How many people work in management positions? **Answer** ☐

Q22 How many women work in manual grades? **Answer** ☐

Q23 Do more men or women work in an administrative role? **Answer** ☐

Q24 What percentage of management positions are filled by men? **Answer** ☐

Q25 Express in its simplest form the ratio between people in managerial grades and people not in managerial grades. **Answer** ☐

Monthly average expenditure for a fictitious household

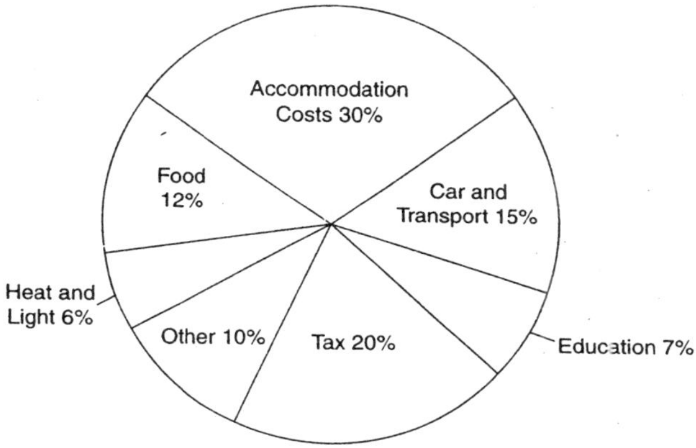

Q26 Does accommodation, education and car and transport account for more than half the family's expenditure?

Yes ☐ No ☐ Cannot tell ☐

Q27 What is the angle of the tax segment? **Answer** ☐

Q28 32% of the family's income is spent on tax and food.

True ☐ False ☐ Cannot tell ☐

Q29 If monthly expenditure on education amounted to $350 what would be the family's annual total expenditure? **Answer** ☐

Q30 If the 10% expenditure on other comprises $180 and it is spent on meals out, newspapers and gifts in the ratio 2:1:6, how much a month does the family spend on gifts? **Answer** ☐

Extracts from the accounts of struggling.com

Notes:
Brackets ( ) indicate loss
All figures are in $000
Gross profit (loss) figures are carried forward. By this it is meant that the $10,000 profit in 2001 is carried forward to the figure for 2002, and the loss in 2002 is carried forward to 2003.

Year	2003	2002	2001
Sales	910	900	?
Expenses	870	?	720
Gross profit (loss)			
Carried forward	20	(20)	10

Q31 Sales for 2003 were 10% higher than sales for 2002.

True ☐ False ☐ Cannot tell ☐

Q32 What was the value of expenses for 2002? **Answer** ☐

Q33 What was the gross profit/loss for the year 2003? **Answer** ☐

Q34 The value for sales in 2001 totalled $730,000.

True ☐ False ☐ Cannot tell ☐

Q35 The gross profit/loss in 2003 was $70,000 more than the 2002 figure.

True ☐ False ☐ Cannot tell ☐

Analysis of contributions to overall gross profit by ore/commodity

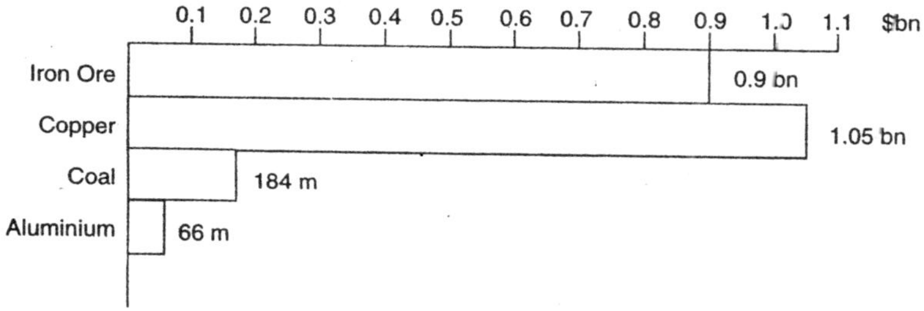

Q36 A billion can be defined as either a thousand million or a million million. Which definition is used in the graph?

1bn = 1 thousand million ☐ 1 bn = 1 million million ☐
Cannot tell ☐

Q37 How much was the total gross profit on the four products? **Answer** ☐

Q38 The gross profits on the sales in coal were based on sales of over 1bn.

True ☐ False ☐ Cannot tell ☐

Q39 Copper and aluminium contributed over half of the gross profit.

True ☐ False ☐ Cannot tell ☐

Q40 If sales for the four commodities totalled $2.95 bn how much was the cost of sales?
(Take gross profit = sales – cost of sales.) **Answer** ☐

Market share

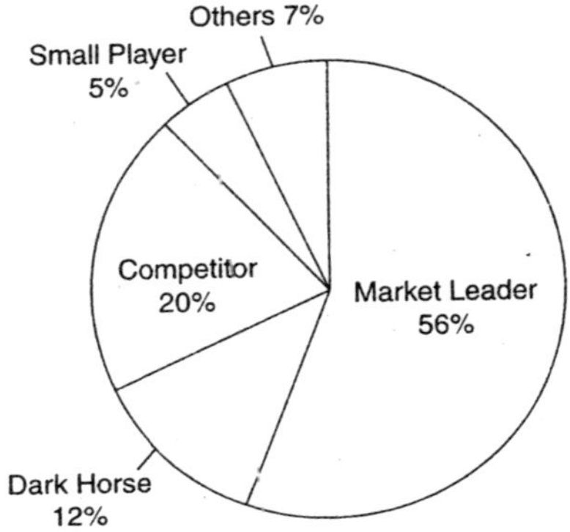

Q41 If Market Leader holds a share of the market worth $112 m what is the value of the whole market? **Answer**

Q42 Express the comparative market shares of Market Leader and Others as a ratio expressed in its simplest form. **Answer**

Q43 How many times bigger than Small Player's share is Competitor's share of the market? **Answer**

Q44 If Small Player was to capture half of Competitor's market how many times bigger would the Small Player share of the market become? **Answer**

Q45 If the market share of Dark Horse is worth $27 m; what is the value of the whole market? **Answer**

Scale of production and unit cost

Note that total costs = fixed costs + variable costs
Unit costs = total costs ÷ output

Outputs per multiple of units	Fixed costs $000	Variable costs $000	Total costs $000	Unit cost
10	?	80	230	23,000
20	150	?	307	15,350
30	150	225	?	12,500
40	150	310	460	?
50	150	370	520	?

Q46 What is the fixed cost for the output of 10 units? **Answer** ☐

Q47 What is the variable cost for the output of 20 units? **Answer** ☐

Q48 What are the total costs for the output of 30 units? **Answer** ☐

Q49 What is the unit cost for 40 units? **Answer** ☐

Q50 How much less is the unit cost for 50 units than for 40 units? **Answer** ☐

Labour and capital productivity

Period	Output	Labour hours	Labour productivity (units per hour)	No of machines	Capital productivity (units per machine)
1	?	875	30	?	5,250
2	29,600	925	?	5	5,920
3	34,500	?	34.5	5	?

Note:
Labour productivity = output ÷ labour hours
Capital productivity = output ÷ no of machines

Q51 What is the output for period 1? **Answer** ☐

Q52 How many machines are in use during period 1? **Answer** ☐

Q53 What is the labour productivity for period 2? **Answer** ☐

Q54 Calculate the labour hours for period 3. **Answer** ☐

Q55 Calculate the capital productivity for period 3. **Answer** ☐

Capacity utilization

Product	Max production 000 items	Actual output 000 items	Capacity utilization %
A	250	225	?
B	150	120	?
C	120	84	70%

Note: actual output ÷ maximum production x 100 = capacity utilization

Q56 What is the maximum output of product A, B and C that can be produced? **Answer** ☐

Q57 How many more units of product C could theoretically be produced? **Answer** ☐

Q58 What is the percentage capacity utilization for product A? **Answer** ☐

Q59 What is the percentage capacity utilization for product B? **Answer** ☐

Q60 Would you expect an increase in the capacity utilization of a product from 90% to 100% to increase or decrease the unit cost?

Increase ☐ Decrease ☐ Cannot tell ☐

Profit and loss

Item	$ 000
Sales turnover	110
Cost of sales	35.2
Gross profit	?
Overheads	37.4
Net profit	?
Tax at 20%	?
Dividend	10
Retained profit	?

Notes
Gross profit = sales turnover – cost of sales
Net profit = sales turnover – cost of sales and overheads
% gross profit = gross profit ÷ sales turnover x 100
% net profit = net profit ÷ sales turnover x 100
Retained profit = net profit – tax – dividend

Q61 What is the gross profit? **Answer** [ ]

Q62 Calculate the net profit. **Answer** [ ]

Q63 Calculate the amount of tax due. **Answer** [ ]

Q64 Calculate the retained profit. **Answer** [ ]

Q65 What is the percentage gross profit? **Answer** [ ]

Budgets verses actual

	Forecast budget $ 000	**Actual $ 000**	**Variance**
Revenue	250	200	-50
Material costs	125	110	+15
Labour costs and overheads	75	70	+5
Net profit	50	?	-30

Note: an adverse variance of actual against budget is indicated with a negative sign while a favourable variance is indicated by a positive sign.

Q66 What percentage of the revenue budget was realized?

Answer

Q67 By what percentage were material costs below budget?

Answer

Q68 What was the actual net profit?

Answer

Q69 What would the actual percentage net profit increase to if an additional $25,000 revenue was realized without incurring any increase in costs?

Answer

Q70 What percentage of the budgeted net profit was realized?

Answer

Cash flow

	Period 1, $ m	Period 2, $ m
Opening balance	0.3	0.13
Sales receipts	1.65	1.5
Collection from aged debt	0.33	0.3
Total cash	2.28	?
Payments		
Tax	0.43	?
Wages net	0.62	0.6
Materials	1.0	1.0
Other costs outgoing	0.1	0.05
Total outgoings	?	1.65
Closing balance	0.13	?

Note: cash flow = sales receipts and collection from aged debt for the period.

Q71 What was total cash for Period 2? **Answer** ☐

Q72 What were the total outgoings for Period 1? **Answer** ☐

Q73 What was the closing balance for Period 2? **Answer** ☐

Q74 How much tax was paid in Period 2? **Answer** ☐

Q75 What was the cash inflow for Period 1? **Answer** ☐

Employment for the month of December 2005

Jobs lost by region	
South	2,000
South East	1,900
South West	?
North	1,100
North East	2,600
North West	700
Total	9,200
Changes in the number of employed by industry (000s)	
Agriculture	+6
Energy	+98
Transport	-20
Finance and business	+3
Education and health	-48
Net total	?

Q76 What is the net total change in the number employed across all industries listed? (State whether the net change is negative or positive.) **Answer** ☐

Q77 How many jobs were lost in the South West during December 2005? **Answer** ☐

Q78 Which two regions account for 50% of the job losses? **Answer** ☐

Q79 If the energy sector had experienced a loss of 98,000 jobs instead of an increase what would be the revised net total? **Answer** ☐

Q80 The North region saw the second lowest number of job losses.

True ☐ False ☐ Cannot tell ☐

Frequency of jobs by sector advertised over a five-day period

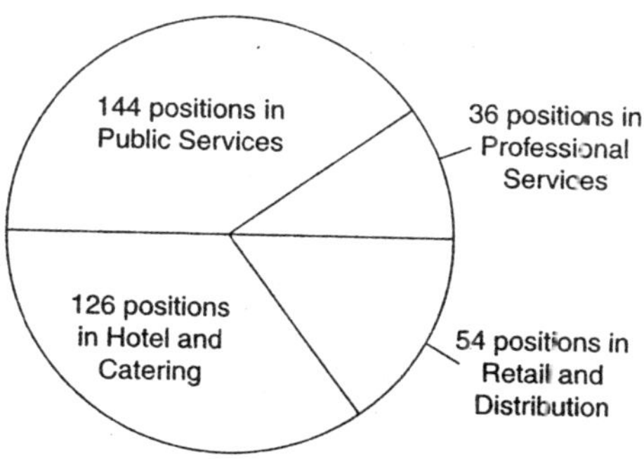

Q81 How many jobs in total were advertised over the five-day period? **Answer** [ ]

Q82 What percentage of the jobs were for positions in retail and distribution? **Answer** [ ]

Q83 More jobs were advertised in public services and professional services than hotel and catering and retail and distribution.

True [ ] False [ ] Cannot tell [ ]

Q84 What percentage of all the jobs were in public services? **Answer** [ ]

Q85 What angle would represent the segment of the pie relating to the 36 professional services positions? **Answer** [ ]

A disappointing summer

Hours of sunshine and percentage comparison with historic averages for August 2003

Hours	% below historic average	Region
306	–15	1
294	–2	2
252	–10	3
222	–40	4
210	–25	5

Q86 Which region experienced the sunniest August 2003? **Answer** [ ]

Q87 How many hours is the historic average for Region 5? **Answer** [ ]

Q88 What percentage of the historic average did Region 4 experience that August? **Answer** ☐

Q89 Does Region 1 or 4 enjoy the higher average historic hours of sunshine? **Answer** ☐

Q90 In Region 2 how many hours below the historic average was August 2003? **Answer** ☐

Number of people celebrating their 100th birthday

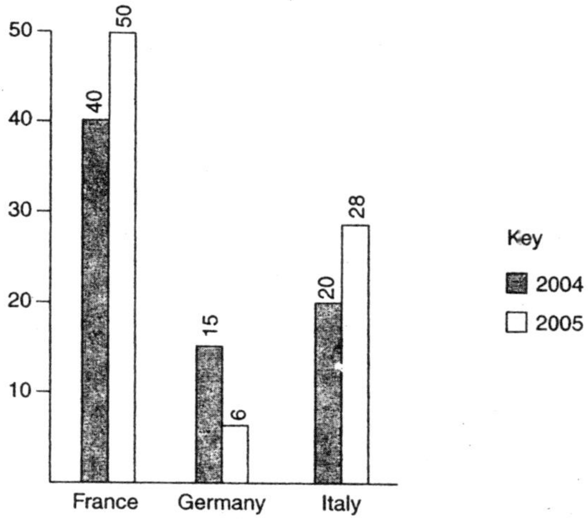

Q91 In the three countries and over the two years 159 people have celebrated their 100th birthdays.

True ☐ False ☐ Cannot tell ☐

Q92 According to the graph do people live longer in France than in Germany? **Answer** ☐

Q93 What is the percentage increase in the number of people celebrating their century between 2004 and 2005 across the three countries? **Answer** ☐

Q94 Over the two years twice as many people celebrated their century in France as in Italy.

True ☐ False ☐ Cannot tell ☐

Q95 60% fewer Germans celebrated their 100th birthday in 2005 than 2004.

True ☐ False ☐ Cannot tell ☐

The balance of power

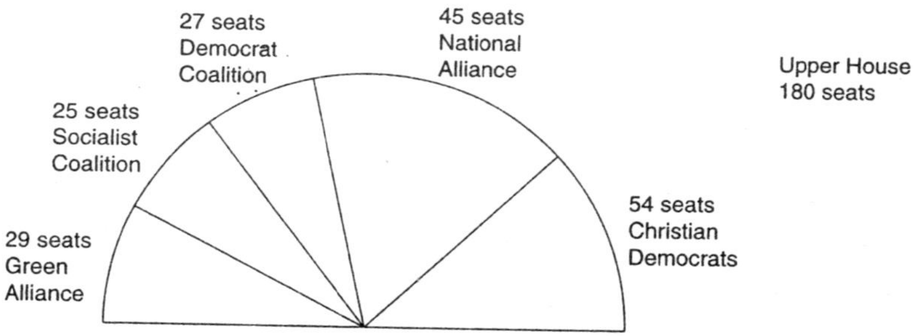

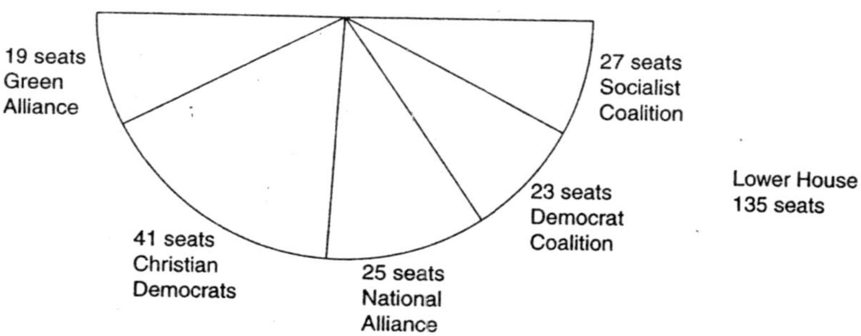

Q96 What percentage of the seats do the Christian Democrats have in the upper house? **Answer** [ ]

Q97 Which two parties if they formed an alliance could gain a majority in the lower house? **Answer** [ ]

Q98 How many seats would a party need to hold in order to have a majority in both houses? **Answer** [ ]

Q99 What percentage of the seats in the upper house do the Green Alliance, Socialist Coalition and Democrat Coalition have between them? **Answer** [ ]

Q100 If at the next election the Democratic Alliance won 1/3 of all the seats in both houses how many seats would it have won? **Answer** [ ]

6

Practise under realistic test conditions to win

In this chapter you will find three realistic practice tests consisting in total of 120 questions (40 per test). These tests are typical of the sorts of numerical test that are in use today. Practise on them to develop your test-taking skills, to build up your speed and accuracy, and your confidence in working under the pressure of time. Make sure that you do not spend too long on any one question, and practise educated guessing (if you do not know the answer to a question, try to rule out some of the suggested answers, then guess from the remaining choices).

To get the most out of your practice and to help make it feel more realistic, set yourself the challenge of trying to beat your own score each time you take one of these practice tests. To do this you will have to try hard and take the challenge seriously; then you will have to try harder still. See how many times you can beat yourself. It's great practice for the real test. Try the following approach:

1. Take the first test against the clock. Stop when the time allowed is over, and mark it and record your score.
2. Now go over the answers and explanations for any questions you got wrong, and try to understand where you went wrong.

3. Set yourself the challenge of beating your first score. Get yourself in the right frame of mind and be ready to 'really go for it' in your second mock test. Take your second mock test, mark your answers and record your score, and see if you did in fact beat your first score.
4. Go over the answers and explanations to your second test and if you got any answers wrong, work out why.
5. Take a third test, trying once again to beat your best score.
6. Record your third score and go over any questions you may have got wrong.
7. Repeat this challenge for each of the practice tests, each time trying to beat your personal best score.

Before you start practising on these realistic tests, make sure you have a number of pencils and some paper to hand for rough working. Note the time, and if possible set an alarm to ring at the time limit of the test so that you stop when the time runs out. Work in a quiet space where you will not be disturbed. Read the instructions first, and go over the practice question and its answer. Concentrate and push yourself to work really hard.

Answers and explanations are provided from page 203 onwards. An interpretation of your score is provided from page 220 onwards.

You will find more practice tests and questions of these types in the following titles from the Kogan Page testing series: *How to Pass Numeracy Tests* by Harry Tolley and Ken Thomas, *How to Pass Numerical Reasoning Tests* by Heidi Smith, and *The Ultimate Psychometric Test Book* by Mike Bryon.

Test 1 Number problems

This test consists of 40 questions, and you are allowed 60 minutes in which to attempt them. You will need to work quickly and not spend too long on any one question.

For each question a box is provided in which to record your answer.

Do not use a calculator.

Attempt all questions, or as many as possible in the time allowed, and work without interruption or pause. When you reach the end of each page, turn over to continue to answer the remaining questions.

When 60 minutes have passed, stop immediately and put your pencil down.

Do not turn over the page until you are ready to begin.

Q1 If the price of a barrel of crude oil increases from $45 to $80.1, what is this increase expressed as a percentage?

Answer [ ]

Q2 If the temperature was to rise by 1.20 during the day from the night-time temperature of 0.60, what is the night time temperature as a percentage of the daytime one? (Give your answer to the nearest whole percentage.)

Answer [ ]

Q3 An insurance company sells 2,500 policies and prices them on the assumption that there will be 300 claims. In fact 8% of the policies result in a claim; is this an increase or decrease on the assumed number of claims?

Answer [ ]

Q4 If the number of daylight hours increases from a winter low of 5 to a summer high of 20, what is this increase expressed as a percentage?

Answer [ ]

Q5 If you were to set off to a meeting at 7.42 and arrive at 9.00, then leave one hour and five minutes later and arrive home at 11.50, for how many hours and minutes would you be travelling?

Answer [ ]

Q6 In year 1 a company sold 5,000 units and product A accounted for 30% of these sales. The following year the company sold 1,455 units of product A. How many fewer units did the company sell of product A in the second year?

Answer [ ]

Q7 If an overdraft facility was to be increased from $10,000 to $90,000 what would this increase be in percentage terms?

Answer [ ]

Q8 How many $20 bills would add up to one million, two hundred and fifty thousand dollars?

Answer [ ]

Q9 If the Rainbow Party candidate received 55% of 20,000 votes, how many votes did the other candidates receive?

Answer [ ]

Q10 If a stopping train takes 18.5% longer to complete the same journey than the express which is timetabled to take 3 hours and 20 minutes, how long does the stopping train take?

Answer [ ]

Q11 If an alloy includes 40% of one metal, how many grams of this metal are present in a 3 kg ingot of the alloy?

Answer [ ]

Q12 Wage costs (1/2 of the subcategory) followed by taxation (1/6) and research and development (1/3) together make up a subcategory of 2/3 of a company's expenditure. What fraction of the total expenditure does the wage bill represent?

Answer [ ]

Q13 If a plane in timetabled to leave at 13.40 but is delayed by 55 minutes and arrives at 17.05, how long is the flight? (Give your answer in hours and minutes.)

Answer [ ]

Q14 If the GNP (gross national product) per head of Brazil is $3,020, Japan $21,450, Ethiopia $2,112 and the UK $10,418, what is the average GNP per head for these four countries? **Answer** ☐

Q15 If a small bottle of butane gas weighs 9 kg and a large bottle approximately 45% more, what is the weight of the large bottle? **Answer** ☐

Q16 If you were to start a journey at 06.43 and arrive at 14.08, how many hours and minutes would you have been travelling? **Answer** ☐

Q17 If the average number of days lost to sickness by a workforce fell 3.5 to 3.08, what is this improvement expressed as a percentage? **Answer** ☐

Q18 If an academic year is 75% of a full year, how many weeks does it include? **Answer** ☐

Q19 If an investment fell in value from $4,500 to $2,700 what is this fall in percentage terms? **Answer** ☐

Q20 If 3/5 of a company's income comes from its best-selling product and 1/2 of the remaining income is derived from licences for the production of that product overseas, what fraction of the company's total income is derived from other sources? **Answer** ☐

Q21 If the return from an investment was to increase from 36 to 57.6, what is this improvement expressed as a percentage? **Answer** ☐

Q22 If the mean temperature for a location is 26 degrees and the temperature range is 2 degrees, what are the highest and lowest temperatures experienced at the location? **Answer** ☐

Q23 If a workaholic manages to spend 75% of his time working, how many hours does he work in a week? **Answer** ☐

Q24 1/3 of the 180 homes to be built on a new site are reserved for workers in essential industries, a further 2/5 are designated for homeless families, and the remainder are to be sold on the open market. How many homes are to be sold? **Answer** ☐

Q25 If an athlete is able to improve on his personal best of 1 minute 20 seconds by 7 % what will his new personal best be? **Answer** ☐

Q26 If a meeting begins at 08.42 and finishes at 11.07 and is attended by 5 people, how many hours and minutes in total did the attendees spend away from their desks? **Answer** ☐

Q27 If the value of a company's bad debt was to increase from 4,500 to 4,635, what would this increase represent in percentage terms? **Answer** ☐

Q28 How many minutes do you have if you add 30% of an hour to 45% of an hour? **Answer** ☐

Q29 If location A experiences the highest temperature of 18°, and the lowest temperature of 4°, a temperature range of 14° and rainfall of 585 mm, what is the mean temperature for the location?

Answer ☐

Q30 If a delivery must arrive at 12 noon and the messenger leaves at 7.50 and takes 4 hours and 17 minutes to complete the journey; how late will the delivery be?

Answer ☐

Q31 If 20% of an 18.3 km stretch of road is found to be substandard and in need of repair how many metres of road need to be remade?

Answer ☐

Q32 If a product generates a loss of $1,200 with operating costs of $16,200, what is the percentage loss of total revenue?

Answer ☐

Q33 If the fulfilment time for an order worsens from 5 days to 8 days, what is this increase in percentage terms?

Answer ☐

Q34 1/5 of a workforce travel 10 minutes or less to work, a further 3/8 travel between 10 and 30 minutes to work, while the remainder travel for over 30 minutes. What fraction of the workers travel for more than 30 minutes?

Answer ☐

Q35 If you begin working on an assignment at 08.05, break to take a call lasting 9 minutes, have lunch over a 30-minute period and conclude work on the assignment at 18.30, for how many hours and minutes can you bill the client?

Answer ☐

Q36 If 2/3 of a workforce of 360 are women but only 1/10 of them are in managerial positions or have directorships, how many women are in these senior positions? **Answer** ☐

Q37 If during a period of economic growth 16 sales calls per 1,000 were successful but during a period of recession this rate dropped to 4 calls per thousand; what is this change expressed as a percentage? **Answer** ☐

Q38 If 1/4 of the respondents to a survey indicated that they used a particular product and of these 3/8 reported that they used that product regularly, and in total 4,800 respondents took part in the survey, how many of these were regular users of the product? **Answer** ☐

Q39 What is the percentage decrease in time between 2/3 and 1/6 of an hour? **Answer** ☐

Q40 If the rate of successful proposals fell from 1 in 5 to 1 in 8, what is the percentage decrease in winning bids? **Answer** ☐

End of test

Test 2 Sequencing

This test consists of 40 questions and you are allowed 30 minutes in which to attempt them.

For each question, write the answer in the answer box.

You are not allowed to use a calculator.

Attempt all questions, or as many as possible in the time allowed, and work without interruption or pause. When you reach the end of each page, turn over to continue to answer the remaining questions.

When 30 minutes have passed, stop immediately and put your pencil down.

Do not turn over the page until you are ready to begin.

Q1 ?, 3, 7, 21 Answer

Q2 48, ?, 64, 72 Answer

Q3 168, 126, 91, ?, 42 Answer

Q4 69, 90, ?, 135 Answer

Q5 132, 144, ?, 168 Answer

Q6 12, ?, -3, -9 Answer

Q7 79, 49, ?, 4, -11 Answer

Q8 2500, ?, 1, 0.02 Answer

Q9 21, 14, 7, ? Answer

Q10 23, 29, ?, 37, 41 Answer

Q11 264, 198, 143, ?, 66 Answer

Q12 ?, 321, 421, 522 Answer

Q13 5, 1, 0.2, ? Answer

Q14 ?, 54, 48, 42 Answer

Q15 88, 99, ?, 121 Answer

Q16 81, ?, 58, 45 Answer

Q17 ?, 284, 236, 200, 176 Answer

Q18 1, 3, ?, 15 **Answer** ☐

Q19 45, ?, 35, 27, 17 **Answer** ☐

Q20 8, 110, 213, ? **Answer** ☐

Q21 4096, 1024, ?, 64 **Answer** ☐

Q22 64, 56, 48, ? **Answer** ☐

Q23 ?, 77, 84, 91 **Answer** ☐

Q24 21, 19, 18, ? **Answer** ☐

Q25 84, 60, 42, ?, 24 **Answer** ☐

Q26 1, 2, 5, ? **Answer** ☐

Q27 36, 63, ?, 120 **Answer** ☐

Q28 0.008, 0.2, 5, ? **Answer** ☐

Q29 ?, 66, 55, 44 **Answer** ☐

Q30 24, 27, ?, 33 **Answer** ☐

Q31 300, 200, ?, -3 **Answer** ☐

Q32 ?, 78, 60, 45, 33 **Answer** ☐

Q33 36, ?, 1296, 7776 **Answer** ☐

Q34 14, ?, 37, 50 **Answer** ☐

Q35 0.16, ?, 1, 2.5 **Answer** [ ]

Q36 27, 18, 9, ? **Answer** [ ]

Q37 48, ?, 72, 84 **Answer** [ ]

Q38 ?, 69, 40, 12 **Answer** [ ]

Q39 72, 47, ?, 12, 2 **Answer** [ ]

Q40 1, 2, 3, 4, ?, 8, 12, 24 **Answer** [ ]

End of test

Test 3 Data interpretation

This test consists of 40 questions, and you are allowed 60 minutes in which to attempt them. To complete these questions in the time allowed you must work quickly and not spend too long on any one question.

In this test there are a total of 8 sets of data, presented in tables, graphs or charts. Five questions follow each table, graph or chart. It is your task to use the information provided to answer the questions. It is important that you refer only to that information. For some questions suggested answers are given from which you must select one; for other questions no suggested answers are given. For each question there is an answer box in which you must record your short answer to the question.

You are not allowed to use a calculator.

Attempt all questions, or as many as possible in the time allowed, and work without interruption or pause. When you reach the end of each page, turn over to continue to answer the remaining questions.

When 60 minutes have passed, stop immediately and put your pencil down.

Do not turn over the page until you are ready to begin.

Sales of bullion by the ounce and the sums raised

Year	Average $ unit price	Units sold	Amount raised $ (000s)
2000	270	200	54
2001	?	250	68.75
2002	273	?	40.95
2003	290	300	?

Q1 How much was raised in 2003? **Answer** ☐

Q2 How many units were sold in 2002? **Answer** ☐

Q3 What was the average unit price in 2001? **Answer** ☐

Q4 What was the average unit price over the four years? **Answer** ☐

Q5 How much more would the units sold in 2000 have raised had they been sold in 2003? **Answer** ☐

Expenditure of a small manufacturing company

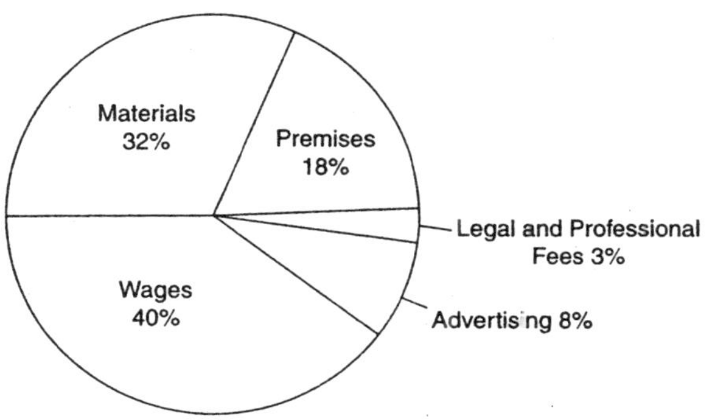

Q6 What percentage of expenditure goes on advertising, legal and professional fees and premises? **Answer** ☐

Q7 If expenditure totals $900,000 how much will the wage bill be? **Answer** ☐

Q8 Which two items of expenditure account for half of the total? **Answer** ☐

Q9 What is the angle of the wages segment of the pie graph? **Answer** ☐

Q10 What is the ratio between expenditure on materials and wages expressed in its simplest form? **Answer** ☐

Extracts from a financial statement for a small business

Brackets ( ) indicate loss or expense. All figures are in $.

Continuing operations	2004	2003
Sales	?	940,100
Cost of sales	(668,990)	(770,882)
Gross profit	211,260	169,218
Administrative expenses	(184,260)	(174,218)
Operating profit (loss)	27,000	?

Q11 What was the value of sales for 2004? Answer ☐

Q12 What was the operating profit or loss for 2003? Answer ☐

Q13 The improvement from a loss to a profit between the years 2003 and 2004 was mainly achieved by improving the level of sales.

True ☐ False ☐ Cannot tell ☐

Q14 As a percentage of sales, gross profit improved between the years 2003 and 2004.

True ☐ False ☐ Cannot tell ☐

Q15 Operating profits in 2004 were less than 3% of sales.

True ☐ False ☐ Cannot tell ☐

International tourists worldwide and by region

Region	2006 world share (%)	1996 world share (%)	Annual growth (%)
World	100	100	
Americas	20	21	0.6
Africa	4	3	7.5
Asia	10	15	-1.2
Europe	65	59	14.5
Middle East	1	2	2.6

Q16 How many regions saw an increase in their share of world tourism between 1996 and 2006?

1 ☐ 2 ☐ 3 ☐ 4 ☐ Cannot tell ☐

Q17 In 2006 what share of world tourism did the rest of the world enjoy (ie regions not included in the list Americas, Africa, Asia, Europe and Middle East)?

0% ☐ 3% ☐ 4% ☐ Cannot tell ☐

Q18 Which region suffered the biggest percentage drop in its share of world tourism?

Americas ☐ Africa ☐ Asia ☐ Europe ☐

Middle East ☐ Cannot tell ☐

Q19 What was the average annual growth for tourism across the five regions between 1996 and 2006?

Answer ☐

Q20 The number of tourists visiting the Middle East in 2006 has decreased in real terms since 1996.

True ☐ False ☐ Cannot tell ☐

Pie graphs comparing employment by industrial sector in two regions

Region 1

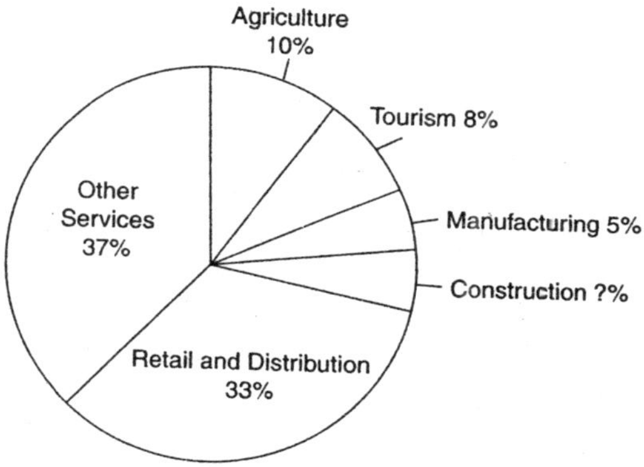

Region 2

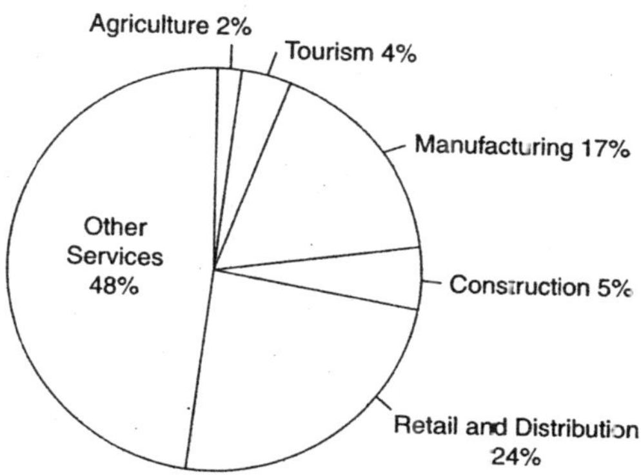

Q21 In Region 1 what percentage of the total are employed in construction? **Answer** ☐

Q22 There are likely to be more gift shops, cafés and restaurants in Region 1 than Region 2.

True ☐ False ☐ Cannot tell ☐

Q23 If 800,000 people work in agriculture in Region 2, how many people work in construction in that region? **Answer** ☐

Q24 In real terms a greater number of people work in tourism in region 1 than 2.

True ☐ False ☐ Cannot tell ☐

Q25 For Region 1 what is the angle for the segment of the pie graph for the percentage of people employed in retail and distribution?

120° ☐ 90° ☐ 45° ☐ 270° ☐

Indicators of development

Country	Birth rate per 1,000	Death rate per 1,000	Life expectancy (years)	Patients per doctor	Literacy rates(%)
1	46	11.5	51	37,000	30
2	25.8	7	66	2,500	45
3	10	8	82	800	99
4	12	13	81	623	97

Q26 Which country has the most doctors?

1 ☐ 2 ☐ 3 ☐ 4 ☐ Cannot tell ☐

Q27 How many more babies are born per 1,000 of the population in Country 4 than in Country 3? **Answer** ☐

Q28 What is the ratio of births and deaths per 1,000 of the population for Country 1 expressed in its simplest form? **Answer** ☐

Q29 Which country has the highest infant mortality rate? **Answer** ☐

Q30 Excluding issues such as immigration and migration, which country whose population is growing is doing so the slowest? **Answer** ☐

Monthly average levels of rainfall and temperature for three regions of Europe

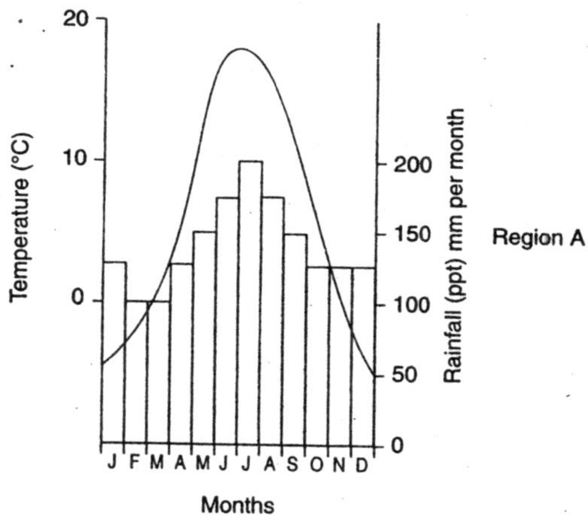

Key
Bar Chart = Rainfall
Line Chart = Average Temperature

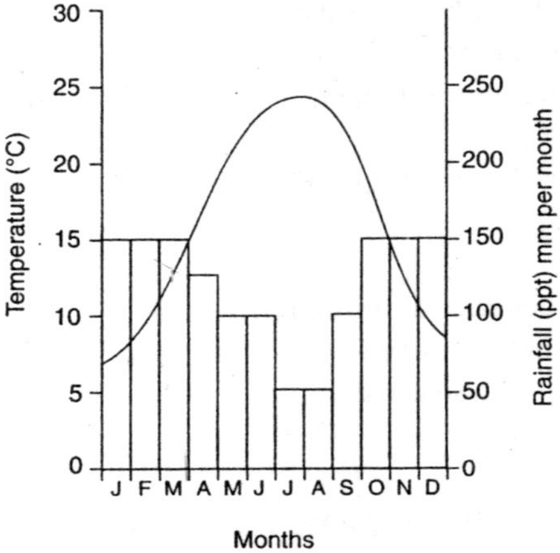

Region B

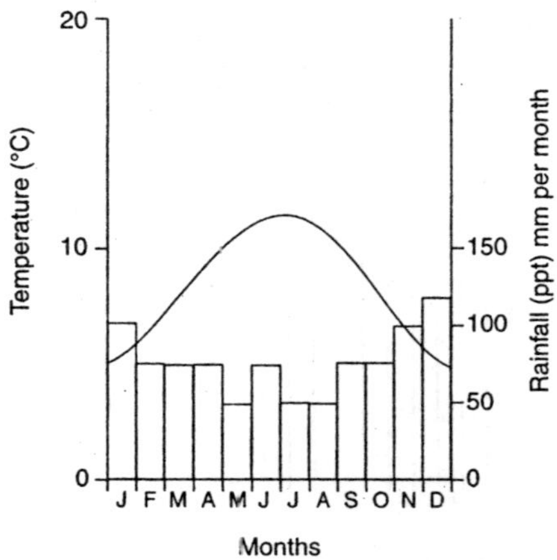

Region C

Key
Bar Chart = Rainfall
Line Chart = Average Temperature

Q31 Which graph best fits a region that enjoys a long hot summer?

A ☐ B ☐ C ☐

Q32 In which region is snowfall most likely to occur?

A ☐ B ☐ C ☐

Q33 Which graph best describes a region that has relatively cool summers and relatively mild winters?

A ☐ B ☐ C ☐

Q34 Which region has the highest level of precipitation?

A ☐ B ☐ C ☐

Q35 Which region experiences the widest temperature range?

A ☐ B ☐ C ☐

Gender and age cohort of a population

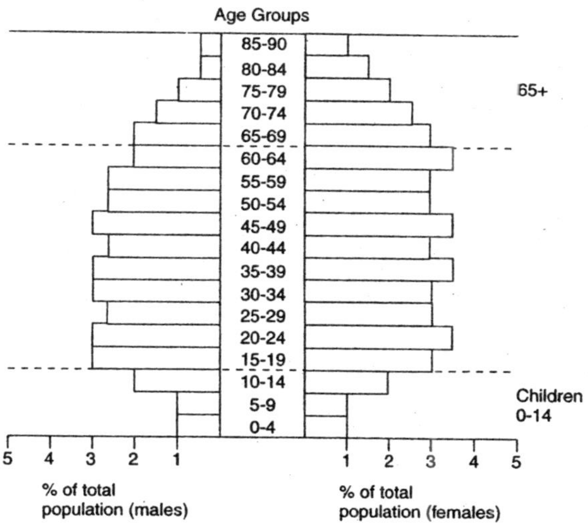

Q36 Do more men or women make up the 65+ group?

Men ☐ Women ☐ Cannot tell ☐

Q37 The narrow base to the graph suggests a high proportion of children as a percentage of the total population.

True ☐ False ☐ Cannot tell ☐

Q38 The total population has been divided into three broad age ranges; what is the age range of the middle cohort?

14–65 ☐ 15–64 ☐ 15–65 ☐ Cannot tell ☐

Q39 What percentage of the total population are children aged 0–9 years?

2% ☐ 4% ☐ 6% ☐ 8% ☐

Q40 Would you expect a person born in this country to have a long or short life expectancy?

Long ☐ Short ☐ Cannot tell ☐

End of test

Answers and detailed explanations

Chapter 2

Quick test 1

Q1 Answer 65

Q2 Answer 96
Explanation: if you cannot immediately get this answer then try breaking the sum into more convenient parts, eg 117 – 20 = 97 – 1 = 96.

Q3 Answer 155
Explanation: see if it helps you to do this sum quickly by doubling 80 and taking away 5.

Q4 Answer 77

Q5 Answer 67

Q6 Answer True
Explanation: 20% is the same as the fraction 20/100, which cancels down to 1/5 (divide both the top and bottom numbers by 20). Now the sum states that 1/5 is more than 1/8, which you can see is the case.

Q7 Answer 34

Q8 Answer 64

Q9 Answer True
Explanation: the ratio 1 : 3 is the same as the fraction 1/3 which is larger than 1/4.

Q10 Answer 18

Q11 Answer Less
Explanation: convert the ratio to a percentage to compare. 1:4 = 1/4. To make a fraction a percentage multiply by 100 = 1 x 100 = 100 ÷ 4 = 25.

Q12 Answer 109

Q13 Answer 117

Q14 Answer 128

Q15 Answer 91

Q16 Answer False, they are the same
Explanation: 6/20 is equivalent to 3/10, 30% is the same as 30/100 which is equivalent to 3/10.

Q17 Answer 42

Q18 Answer 35

Q19 Answer True

Explanation: they are equivalent fractions as 18/24 cancels down to 6/8 (divide the top and bottom numbers by 3).

Q20 Answer True

Explanation: to convert decimals to fractions simply multiply by 100. 0.05 x 100 = 5.

Q21 Answer 81

Q22 Answer 193

Q23 Answer 181

Q24 Answer 0.2

Explanation: to convert a fraction to a decimal divide the top number of the fraction by the bottom number. 1 ÷ 5 = 0.2.

Q25 Answer 45

Q26 Answer 11

Q27 Answer 3199

Q28 Answer 28

Q29 Answer 1610

Explanation: try doing this faster by treating 390 as 400 and then adding 10. 2000 – 400 = 1600 + 10 = 1610.

Q30 Answer 30

Quick test 2

Q1 Answer 137

Q2 Answer 12
Explanation: 20 ÷ 100 x 60 = 12.

Q3 Answer 13

Q4 Answer True
Explanation: 12.5/100 = 1/8 (12.5 divided into 100 goes 8 times).

Q5 Answer 35

Q6 Answer False
Explanation: 12/15 does not cancel down to 3/4. Its lowest expression is 4/5 (both top and bottom number divided by 3).

Q7 Answer 45

Q8 Answer 153

Q9 Answer 288
Explanation: a quick way to work this out is (12 x 12) x 2, 12 x 12 = 144 x 2 = 288.

Q10 Answer False
Explanation: to do this properly you should change the fractions into equivalents with the same bottom number (denominator). Do this by multiplying the existing denominators 5 x 3 = 15, then express the fractions as equivalents. 12/5 = 36/15 (multiply top and bottom by 3), 8/3 = 40/15 (multiply top and bottom by 5). You can now see which is the greater number. In a quick test however it is faster to estimate, and it helps if you change improper fractions such as these into mixed fractions: 12/5 = 2 2/5, 8/3 = 2 2/3. Now you can see that 8/3 is larger, as 2/3 is larger than 2/5.

Q11 Answer 36

Q12 Answer 23

Q13 Answer 47.5
Explanation: to convert from decimals to percentages simply multiply by 100.

Q14 Answer 72

Q15 Answer 2/5
Explanation: you need to remove the decimal point, so multiply by 10 to give 4/10, which cancels down to 2/5 (divide both numbers by 2).

Q16 Answer 274

Q17 Answer 112

Q18 Answer 60%
Explanation: 3/5 as a decimal = 3 ÷ 5 =.0.6 as a percentage = 0.6 x 100 = 60.

Q19 Answer 75%
Explanation: 3/4 = the decimal 0.75 (3 ÷ 4) x 100 to get the percentage = 75.

Q20 Answer 65

Q21 Answer 20

Q22 Answer 0.125
Explanation: to convert between percentages and decimals multiply the percentage by 100.

Q23 Answer 165
Explanation: work this quickly by calculating 10 x 15 = 150 + 15 = 165.

Q24 Answer 1.2
Explanation: divide a percentage by 100 to convert it to a decimal.

Q25 Answer 18000
Explanation: 6 x 3 = 18, then add the three zeros = 18000.

Q26 Answer 63

Q27 Answer 20%
Explanation: 1 ÷ 5 = 0.2 x 100 = 20.

Q28 Answer 9
Explanation: first find one-tenth of 30 and then multiply it by 3, 30 ÷ 10 = 3 x 3 = 9.

Q29 Answer 200 gm
Explanation: 1 kg comprises 1000 gm, 1/5 of 1000 = 200.

Q30 Answer 82

Q31 Answer True
Explanation: divide the top and bottom number of 8/32 by 8 to get 1/4.

Q32 Answer 24

Q33 Answer 144

Q34 Answer 60 cm
Explanation: 100 cm = 1 metre, 200 cm = 2 metres, 3/10 of 200 = (1/10 = 20 x 3) = 60.

Q35 Answer 98

Q36 Answer 70

Q37 Answer 80
Explanation: 200 ÷ 5 = 40 x 2 = 80

Q38 Answer 1.5
Explanation: one litre = 1,000 cm^3 so 1,500 cm^3 = 1.5 litres.

Q39 Answer True
Explanation: square numbers are 1 x 1 = 1, 2 x 2 = 4, 3 x 3 = 9 and so on. 36 is a square number because it is the product of 6 x 6.

Q40 Answer 380
Explanation: calculate 20 x 20 = 400 and minus 20 = 380.

Q41 Answer True
Explanation: factors are the whole numbers that divide into something exactly. 3 divides into 18 6 times so it is true. All the factors of 18 are 1, 2, 3, 6, 9 and 18.

Q42 Answer 84

Q43 Answer 25

Q44 Answer 3 feet and 6 inches
Explanation: 12 inches make a foot, 3 x 12 = 36 leaving 6 inches = 3 feet, 6 inches.

Q45 Answer 49

Q46 Answer 77

Q47 Answer 42

Q48 Answer 4/5
Explanation: 0.8 x 10 = 8/10 which simplifies to 4/5 (divide both top and bottom by 2).

Q49 Answer 27

Q50 Answer 13

Q51 Answer 200: 100
Explanation: divide the total 300 by the number of parts it must be shared between: 2 + 1 = 3, 300 ÷ 3 = 100, then multiply to calculate each share: 2 x 100 = 200, 1 x 100 = 100.

Q52 Answer 67

Q53 Answer 250
Explanation: we move the decimal point one place to the right for each zero, 10,000 has 4 zeros so 0.025 x 10000 = 250.

Q54 Answer 105
Explanation: you can work this as (10 x 7) = 70 + (5 x 7) = 35 = 105.

Q55 Answer 7

Q56 Answer 300
Explanation: you can do this sum in 5 seconds as long as you divide by the 7 and then add the same number of zeros, 21 ÷ 7 = 3 add 00 = 300.

Q57 Answer 8
Explanation: 1 kg = 1,000 gm, 1000 ÷125 = 8.

Q58 Answer 81

Q59 Answer 94
Explanation: a cubed number is the product of 1x1x1, 2x2x2, 3x3x3 etc. You should learn the first 10. 4x4x4 = 64, 5x5x5 =125 so 94 is not a cubed number.

Q60 Answer 169

Quick test 3

Q1 Answer 18

Q2 Answer 6
Explanation: 12 x 5 = 60 ÷ 10 = 6.

Q3 Answer 15

Q4 Answer A
Explanation: 4 x 4 = 16, 4 x 3 = 12.

Q5 Answer 42

Q6 Answer 48
Explanation: 6 x 8 = 48, 8 x 6 = 48, 12 x 4 = 48

Q7 Answer 31
Explanation: expect the unexpected in a psychometric test! A test author will pose a question that takes you by surprise.

Q8 Answer Less than

Q9 Answer 1984

Q10 Answer 18

Q11 Answer 64
Explanation: $4 \times 4 \times 4 = 64$.

Q12 Answer 100°C

Q13 Answer 12
Explanation: $18 \div 6 = 3 \times 4 = 12$.

Q14 Answer 17

Q15 Answer Equal to or less than

Q16 Answer 3.45

Q17 Answer 4
Explanation: if you multiply 2 by the power of 4 you get 16, $2 \times 2 \times 2 \times 2 = 16$.

Q18 Answer Yes
Explanation: whole number factors (WNF) are those that divide exactly into the number. The WNF of 18 are 1, 2, 3, 6, 9, 18.

Q19 Answer 38

Q20 Answer 500
Explanation: if you gave the answer 1000 then you read the question too quickly, as it asked for the number of grams in half a kilo.

Q21 Answer 900
Explanation: $15 \times 60 = 900$.

Q22 Answer 12.35

Q23 Answer 57

Q24 Answer 20

Q25 Answer No
Explanation: cubed numbers are whole numbers raised to the power of 3. The sequence of cubed numbers starts 1, 8, 27, 64, 125. It is worth learning the sequence as far as 10^3.

Q26 Answer Saturday

Q27 Answer 10
Explanation: to work these sums start with the last given figure and then reverse the sums. Eg work backwards making a division a multiplication, addition a subtraction, like this: 100 ÷ 2 ÷ 5 = 10.

Q28 Answer 800
Explanation: there are 10 mm in a cm.

Q29 Answer Greater than

Q30 Answer 15

Q31 Answer 54
Explanation: 9 x 6 = 54.

Q32 Answer 45 minutes

Q33 Answer 12
Explanation: start with the given last number, reverse the signs and work backwards. 20 x 2 (rather than halve it) = 40 x 3 (rather than divide it) = 120 ÷ 10 (rather than multiply) = 12.

Q34 Answer 6

Q35 Answer 144

Q36 Answer 27

Q37 Answer 0.125
Explanation: obtain the reciprocal value by dividing the number into 1. $1 \div 8 = 0.125$. It pays to know the most common reciprocals.

Q38 Answer 30

Q39 Answer Yes
Explanation: the sequence of square numbers runs 1, 4, 9, 16, 25, 36. It is worth learning.

Q40 Answer 49

Q41 Answer 27
Explanation: 3 to the power of $3 = 3^3 = 3 \times 3 \times 3 = 27$.

Q42 Answer 44

Q43 Answer 1:3
Explanation: these are just like fractions. (Sorry if this comment does not help!) Find the highest whole number that divides exactly into both numbers, in this case 4, then divide both figures. $4 \div 4 = 1$, $12 \div 4 = 3$, so the ratio cancels down to the equivalent 1:3.

Q44 Answer 54
Explanation: the denominator is the lower figure in a fraction. To find an equivalent fraction simply identify the multiple that links the two equivalent numerators (top numbers) and multiply the given denominator by the same value. Eg $2 \times 6 = 12$, so multiply 9×6 to get the missing lower number = 54.

Q45 Answer 208
Explanation: do this quickly by multiplying $50 \times 4 = 200$ plus $2 \times 4 = 8$.

Q46 Answer 0.25

Explanation: to get a number's reciprocal value divide it into 1, 1 ÷ 4 = 0.25.

Q47 Answer 72

Q48 Answer 5

Explanation: squares have sides all the same length, and the length of the sides of a square with an area of 25 m^2 is 5 m. 5^2 is 25.

Q49 Answer 42

Q50 Answer Prime numbers

Explanation: The sequence of the first 5 prime numbers (prime numbers are those that only have 1 and themselves as factors), the sequence of odd numbers that include the number 9.

Q51 Answer 12

Q52 Answer 3.14

Q53 Answer 8

Q54 Answer 18

Explanation: $2^4 = 2 \times 2 \times 2 \times 2 = 16$.

Q55 Answer 6

Q56 Answer 5

Explanation: $18 - 3 = 15$, so $3x = 15$, $x = 5$.

Q57 Answer 7

Q58 Answer 4

Explanation: 1, 2 and 4 all divide exactly into 4, the WNF of 5 are 1, 5. For 6 they are 1, 2, 3, 6.

Q59 Answer 0.2
Explanation: $1 \div 5 = 0.2$

Q60 Answer 2 : 5
Explanation: The highest factor common to both 16 and 40 is 8, $16 \div 8 = 2$, $40 \div 8 = 5$.

Quick test 4

Q1 Answer True

Q2 Answer 55

Q3 Answer False
Explanation: $8 \times 6 = 48$.

Q4 Answer 72

Q5 Answer 19

Q6 Answer False
Explanation: $6 \times 15 = 90$.

Q7 Answer 56

Q8 Answer 199

Q9 Answer 66

Q10 Answer True

Q11 Answer 107

Q12 Answer 42

Q13 Answer True

Explanation: you can do this quickly if you treat this as 200 + 200 + 11 – 2 to get 409.

Q14 Answer 105

Explanation: try doing this more quickly by for example calculating 20 x 5 = 100 + 5 = 105.

Q15 Answer False

Explanation: 139 – 21 = 118.

Q16 Answer A

Q17 Answer 297

Explanation: do this quickly by adding 100 + 200 – 3 = 297.

Q18 Answer 825

Q19 Answer 12

Q20 Answer 963

Q21 Answer 12

Explanation: start at the end and reverse the operations: 7 x 6 = 42 ÷ 7 = 6 x 2 = 12.

Q22 Answer 21,196

Q23 Answer 40

Explanation: start with the number 10 and reverse the sum and operations, 10 x 12 = 120 ÷ 3 = 40.

Q24 Answer 2,157

Q25 Answer 3
Explanation: start with 36 and reverse the signs, 36 ÷ 4 = 9, which is 3 x 3.

Q26 Answer 1104

Q27 Answer 1996
Explanation: do this quickly by for example doubling 1000 then adding 5 and –9 = 1996.

Q28 Answer 7,999
Explanation: do this quickly, minus 2,000 from 10,000 = 8,000, minus 4 from 3 to give you 7,999.

Q29 Answer 591
Explanation: do this quickly by treating each sum as 200 x 3 = 600 – (–2, –3 –4 =) –9 = 591.

Q30 Answer A

Q31 Answer 164
Explanation: do this quickly by for example doubling 77 then adding 10.

Q32 Answer C

Q33 Answer 54

Q34 Answer 10

Q35 Answer 6
Explanation: do this quickly by for example working out 20% of 10 = 2 and multiplying it by 3 = 6.

Q36 Answer 0.334

Q37 Answer 24
Explanation: 40 ÷ 5 = 8 x 3 = 24.

Q38 Answer 0.0349

Q39 Answer 12, 36 and 48

Q40 Answer 75%
Explanation: to convert a fraction to a percentage multiply by 100, 3/4 x 100 = 3 x 100 ÷ 4 = 75.

Q41 Answer 5
Explanation: you should be fast at these by now. Start with 30, reverse all the operations, 30 ÷ 2 = 15÷ 3 = 5.

Q42 Answer 12

Q43 Answer 35 minutes
Explanation: divide 60 by 12 and then multiply it by 7, 60 ÷ 12 = 5 x 7 = 35.

Q44 Answer 0.00045

Q45 Answer 93.2

Q46 Answer 0.04
Explanation: divide by 100, 4/100 = 0.04 (do this quickly by moving the decimal point two places).

Q47 Answer –6
Explanation: replace the signs + – with – then the sum becomes –3 – 3 = –6.

Q48 Answer 0
Explanation: replace – with + then the sum becomes –2 + 2 = 0.

Q49 Answer 8

Q50 Answer –12
Explanation: You can replace the signs – + with the – sign so the sum become –7 – 5 = –12.

Q51 Answer 0

Q52 Answer –17
Explanation: the 3 has a hidden + sign and you can replace the – + signs with the – sign.

Q53 Answer 18
Explanation: replace the – sign with + to get 10 + 8 = 18.

Q54 Answer 7 km
Explanation: divide 63 by 9 = 7 (9 x 7 = 63).

Q55 Answer 40 minutes
Explanation: divide 50 by 5 to get 10 and multiply it by 4 to give 40.

Q56 Answer $4m^2$
Explanation: 10 ÷ 5 = 2 x 2 = 4.

Q57 Answer 1/3

Q58 Answer 2/3

Q59 Answer 5/8

Q60 Answer 1/2

Quick test 5

Q1 Answer 12%
Explanation: to change a fraction into a percentage multiply by 100. 3 x 100 = 300 ÷ 25 = 12.

Q2 Answer 1,500

Explanation: do this quickly by working out how many hundreds there are in 50,000 (500) and then multiplying by 3.

Q3 Answer 6

Explanation: start with 4 and swap the operations; 4 x 12 = 48 ÷ 2 = 24, 24 ÷ 4 = 6.

Q4 Answer 24

Explanation: 8 x 4 = 32 so the equivalent numerator can be found by multiplying 6 x 4 = 24.

Q5 Answer 15%

Explanation: convert 30/200 to an equivalent fraction with a denominator of 100.

Q6 Answer 4.8

Explanation: you can do this quickly by seeing that 8% of 10 = 0.8 x 6 = 4.8.

Q7 Answer 36

Explanation: 3 x 12 = 36, 4 x 9 = 36, 6 x 6 = 36.

Q8 Answer A

Explanation: convert the decimal into an equivalent fraction and then compare. 0.2 = 0.2/1 = 2/10 which simplifies to 1/5, which you can now see is the smallest.

Q9 Answer 16

Explanation: 12 ÷ 6 = 2, x 4 = 8 x 2 = 16.

Q10 Answer 1/5

Explanation: 2/8 simplifies to 1/4 and 0.25 converts to 1/4. Now you can see that 1/5 is smallest.

Q11 Answer 13
Explanation: replace the – – signs with +.

Q12 Answer 10%
Explanation: 10% = 1/10, 0.33 = 1/3. Now you can see that 10% is the smallest.

Q13 Answer 8
Explanation: 1/3 x 24 = 24 ÷ 3 = 8.

Q14 Answer 0.3
Explanation: 0.3 = 3/10 which you can see is larger than 3/12.

Q15 Answer 560
Explanation: do this quickly by multiplying 40 x 4 = 160 + 400 = 560.

Q16 Answer 50%
Explanation: 0.4 = 40%, 2/5 = 2 x 100 ÷ 5 = 40% also, so 50% is largest.

Q17 Answer 108
Explanation: 18% is 18 in every 100 so 18 x 6 = 18% of 600 = 108.

Q18 Answer 44%
Explanation: multiply a decimal by 100 to convert it to a percentage: 0.44 x 100 = 44.

Q19 Answer 4/5
Explanation: divide by 100, 80/100. To cancel it down, find the highest common factor which is 20, so the fraction cancels to 4/5.

Q20 Answer C
Explanation: multiply the decimal by 100 and do this by moving the decimal point to the right. 0.01 x 100 = 1.

Q21 Answer 11
Explanation: replace – – with + to give 2 + 9 = 11.

Q22 Answer 1/4
Explanation: divide the percentage by 100, 25/100 cancels to 1/4 (the highest common factor is 25).

Q23 Answer 32
Explanation: start with 20 and reverse the operations. 20 ÷ 5 = 4 x 2 = 8 x 4 = 32.

Q24 Answer 30%
Explanation: Multiply by 100, 3/10 x 100 = 3 x 100 = 300 ÷ 10 = 30.

Q25 Answer 480
Explanation: 2 minutes = 120 seconds x 4 = 480.

Q26 Answer 25%
Explanation: multiply by 100, 5 x 100 = 500 ÷ 20 = 25.

Q27 Answer 0.7
Explanation: divide by 100, 70 ÷ 100 = 0.7.

Q28 Answer 0.83
Explanation: convert the percentage to a decimal by dividing by 100 and then compare, 63 ÷ 100 = 0.63 which is smaller than the decimal 0.83.

Q29 Answer 0.45
Explanation: divide the percentage by 100. Do this by moving the decimal point two places to the left.

Q30 Answer 6
Explanation: replace the – – sign with a + to give the sum –4 + 10 = 6.

Q31 Answer 12.5%
Explanation: convert and compare, 12.5% = the fraction 12.5/100 = 1/8 (HCF 12.5).

Q32 Answer 19.01

Q33 Answer 125 km
Explanation: 50 x 2.5 = 125.

Q34 Answer 0.91

Q35 Answer 1.08

Q36 Answer 4
Explanation: approximate this sort of sum by treating 27 as 25 and 108 as 100.

Q37 Answer 360
Explanation: 30% = 30 in every hundred, 1200 = 12 hundreds so 30% of 1200 = 30 x 12 = 360.

Q38 Answer 30
Explanation: do this quickly by treating 900 as 9 (3 x 3 = 9) so 30 x 30 = 900.

Q39 Answer 120

Q40 Answer 9

Q41 Answer 15.24

Q42 Answer B
Explanation: You should be quick at these by now. 20 ÷ 5 = 4, 2 x 2 = 4 so the answer is 2.

Q43 Answer 750 gm
Explanation: 1 kg = 1000 gm, 3/4 of 1000 = 750.

Q44 Answer 36 and 24

Q45 Answer 190

Q46 Answer –11
Explanation: replace the signs – + with – to make the sum –2 – 9 = –11.

Q47 Answer 9

Q48 Answer 11

Q49 Answer 8.1

Q50 Answer 4
Explanation: replace + – with –.

Q51 Answer False
Explanation: you should be able to estimate this and realize quickly that it is false. 20% = 1/5 and 1/5 of 25 = 5 so 20% of 24 must be less not more than 5 km.

Q52 Answer 5
Explanation: replace the signs – – with a + to make the sum –4 + 9 = 5.

Q53 Answer 77
Explanation: 77 divided by 7 = 11.

Q54 Answer 25
Explanation: 30 ÷ 6 = 5 x 5 = 25.

Q55 Answer 5.1

Q56 Answer 72
Explanation: 72 divided by 8 = 9.

Q57 Answer 600 ml
Explanation: 1 litre = 1,000 ml x 6/10 = 600.

Q58 Answer 36
Explanation: 4 x 9 = 36, 6 x 6 = 36.

Q59 Answer –9
Explanation: replace the + – signs with a – to make the sum –2 – 7 = –9.

Q60 Answer 190

Chapter 3

The first 40 questions

Add the same number

Example question

Q1 2, 4, 6, 8, ? Answer 10
Explanation: at each step 2 is added.

Q2 Answer 30
Explanation: 6 is added each step starting with 3 x 6 = 18.

Q3 Answer 55
Explanation: at each step 11 is added, starting with 11 x 5 = 55.

Q4 Answer 72
Explanation: at each step 9 is added, beginning with 9 x 7 = 63.

Q5 Answer 77

Explanation: 7 is added each step, starting with 10 x 7 = 70.

Subtract the same number

Worked example

Q6 12, 10, 8, ? Answer 6

Explanation: subtract 2 each step starting with 2 x 6 = 12.

Q7 Answer 42

Explanation: subtract 6 each step starting with 9 x 6 = 54.

Q8 Answer 42

Explanation: subtract 7 each step starting with 7 x 7 = 49.

Q9 Answer 18

Explanation: subtract 3 each step starting with 9 x 3 = 27.

Q10 Answer 108

Explanation: subtract 12 each step beginning with 12 x 11 = 132.

Multiply or divide by the same number

Worked example

Q11 4, 8, 16, ? Answer 32

Explanation: the previous number is multiplied by 2 each step.

Q12 Answer 125

Explanation: at each step divide the previous number by 5.

Q13 Answer 81

Explanation: multiply the previous number by 3 each step, 27 x 3 = 81.

Q14 Answer 256

Explanation: at each step the previous number is multiplied by 2, 128 x 2 = 256.

Q15 Answer 216
Explanation: multiply the previous number each step by 6, 36 x 6 = 216.

Add a changing number

Worked example

Q16 2, ?, 9, 14 Answer 5
Explanation: 3 is added at the first step to give 5, then 4 is added to give 9, then 5 to give 14.

Q17 Answer 16
Explanation: 4 is added to 16 to make 20, then 5 is added to get 25, then 6 to get 31.

Q18 Answer 36
Explanation: add 1 to make 31, then 2 to make 33, then 3 to get 36.

Q19 Answer 22
Explanation: add 5 to get 22, then 6 to get 28, then 7 to get 35.

Q20 Answer 201
Explanation: add 50 to 100 to get 150, then 51 to get 201, then 52 to get 253.

Subtract a changing number

Worked example

Q21 45, ?, 34, 30 Answer 39
Explanation: 45 (– 6), 39 (–5), 34 (–4), 30.

Q22 Answer 4
Explanation: 9 (–3), 6 (– 2), 4 (– 1), 3.

Q23 Answer 27
Explanation: 27 (– 7), 20 (– 8), 12 (– 9), 3.

Q24 Answer 57
Explanation: 99 (– 15), 84 (– 14), 70 (– 13), 57.

Q25 Answer 21
Explanation: 21 (– 3), 18 (– 2), 16 (– 1), 15.

A sequence of multiples

Worked example

Q26 100, ?, 115, 130, 150 Answer 105
Explanation: 100 (+ 5x1), 105 (+ 5x2), 115 (+ 5x3), 130 (+ 5x4), 150.

Q27 Answer 21
Explanation: 7 (+ 3x2), 13 (+ 4x2), 21 (+ 5x2), 31 (+ 6x2), 43.

Q28 Answer 16
Explanation: 16 (+ 2x4=8), 24 (+ 3x4=12), 36 (+ 4x4=16), 52 (+ 5x4=20), 72.

Q29 Answer 25
Explanation: 7 (+ 3x1=3), 10 (+ 3x2=6), 16 (+ 3x3=9,) 25 (+ 3x4=12), 37.

Q30 Answer 20
Explanation: 10 (+ 1x10=10), 20 (+ 2x10=20), 40 (+ 3x10=30), 70 (+ 4x10=40), 110.

A sequence of multiples in reverse

Worked example

Q31 102, 90, 72, ?, 18 Answer 48
Explanation: 102 (– 6x2=12), 90 (– 6x3=18), 72 (– 6x4=24), 48 (– 6x5=30), 18.

Q32 Answer 60
Explanation: 68 (– 2x4=8), 60 (– 2x5=10), 50 (– 2x6=12), 38 (– 2x7=14), 24.

Q33 Answer 38
Explanation: 42 (– 4x1=4), 38 (– 4x2=8), 30 (– 4x3=12), 18 (– 4x4=16), 2.

Q34 Answer 90
Explanation: 140 (– 10x2=20), 120 (– 10x3=30), 90 (– 10x4=40),50 (– 10x5=50), 0.

Q35 Answer 110
Explanation: 131 (– 7x3=21), 110 (– 8x3=24), 86 (– 9x3=27), 59 (– 10x3=30), 29.

Sequences that test your knowledge of factors, powers and prime numbers

Worked example

Q36 2, 3, 5, ? Answer 7
Explanation: these are the first four numbers in the series of prime numbers. (These are numbers that only have two whole number factors, 1 and themselves, ie 2 is divisible only by the whole numbers 1 and 2. It is also the only even prime number.)

Q37 Answer 27
Explanation: this is the series of cubed numbers beginning with 1x1x1=1, 2x2x2=8, 3x3x3=27, 4x4x4=64.

Q38 Answer 3
Explanation: this is the series of factors of 6 (factors are whole number multiples of a number that leaves no remainders, i.e. 1x6=6, 2x3=6, 6x1=6.

Q39 Answer 81
Explanation: this is the series of 3 raised to the power of 2, 3, 4, 5, 6 ie 3x3=9, 3x3x3=27, 3x3x3x3=81, 3x3x3x3x3=243, 3^6=729.

Q40 Answer 25

Explanation: this is the series of 5 raised by the powers 2, 3, 4, 5 ie $5^2=25$, $5^3=125$, $5^4=625$, $5^5=3125$.

160 more number sequence questions

Q41 Answer 21

Explanation: five is added to the previous number at each step in the series.

Q42 Answer 15

Explanation: these are the factors of 30: 1x30, 2x15, 3x10, 5x6, 6x5, 10x3, 15x2, 30x1.

Q43 Answer 99

Explanation: 198(– 6x9=54), 144 (– 5x9=45), 99 (– 4x9=36), 63.

Q44 Answer 21

Explanation: 7 is added each step starting with 7x3=21.

Q45 Answer 60

Explanation: 60 (– 10), 50 (– 9), 41 (– 8), 33

Q46 Answer 99

Explanation: 50(+ 7x7=49), 99 (+ 8x7=56), 155 (+ 9x7=63), 218.

Q47 Answer 22

Explanation: add 3 to the previous number at each step in the series.

Q48 Answer 1

Explanation: this is the list of factors for 8, and the missing factor is 1. They are 1x8=8, 2x4=8, 4x2=8, 8x1=8.

Q49 Answer 4

Explanation: this is the first five numbers in the series of square numbers (whole numbers raised to the power of 2). It is worth learning them: they continue 1, 4, 16, 25, 36, 49, 81.

Q50 Answer 72

Explanation: subtract 9 from the previous sum each step, beginning with 9x11=99.

Q51 Answer 8

Explanation: at each step the previous sum is divided by 2, 16 ÷ 2 = 8.

Q52 Answer 47

Explanation: 11+11= 22, 22 +12= 34, 34 + 13 = 47.

Q53 Answer 158

Explanation: add 12 to the previous number.

Q54 Answer 138

Explanation: 70 (+ 8x4= 32), 102 (+ 9x4=36), 138 (+ 10x4=40), 178 (+ 11x4=44), 222.

Q55 Answer 105

Explanation: 30 (+ 7x5=35), 65 (+ 8x5=40), 105 (+ 9x5=45), 150 (+ 10x5=50), 200.

Q56 Answer 128

Explanation: this is the series of 2 raised by the powers 2^5, 2^6, 2^7, 2^8 = 128.

Q57 Answer 64

Explanation: 32 (+ 8x4=32), 64 (+ 8x5=40), 104 (+ 8x6=48), 152 (+ 8x7=56), 208.

Q58 Answer 14
Explanation: 33 (– 9), 24 (– 10), 14 (– 11), 3.

Q59 Answer 36
Explanation: the previous number is multiplied by 3.

Q60 Answer 112
Explanation: 40(+ 3x7=21), 61(+ 3x8=24), 85 (+ 3x9=27), 112 (+ 3x10=30), 142.

Q61 Answer 13
Explanation: this is part of the series of prime numbers which runs 2, 3, 5, 7, 11, 13, 17, 19, 23, 29, 31, 37, 41...

Q62 Answer 108
Explanation: 66 (+ 6x3=18), 84 (+ 6x4=24), 108(+ 6x5=30), 138 (+ 6x6=36), 174.

Q63 Answer –13
Explanation: 200 (– 70), 130 (– 71), 59 (– 72), –13.

Q64 Answer 169
Explanation: 25 (+ 3x12=36), 61 (+ 4x12=48), 109 (+ 5x12=60), 169 (+ 6x12=72), 241.

Q65 Answer 10
Explanation: the previous number is multiplied by 2.

Q66 Answer 1
Explanation: multiply the previous number by 3 each step.

Q67 Answer 45
Explanation: subtract 5 from the previous number each step beginning with 5x9=45.

Q68 Answer 21
Explanation: 21(+ 7x10=70), 91 (+ 8x10=80), 171 (+ 9x10=90), 261.

Q69 Answer 81
Explanation: this is the series of 9 raised by the powers $9^1, 9^2, 9^3, 9^4$ = 9x1=9, 9x9=81, 9x9x9=729, 9^4 = 6561.

Q70 Answer 44
Explanation: 24(+ 5x4=20), 44 (+ 6x4=24), 68 (+ 7x4=28), 96 (+ 8x4=32), 128.

Q71 Answer 100,000
Explanation: the previous number is multiplied by 10.

Q72 Answer 60
Explanation: 12 is added to the previous sum each step starting with 12x6=36.

Q73 Answer 106
Explanation: 22(+ 3x7=21), 43 (+ 4x7=28), 71 (+ 5x7=35), 106 (+ 6x7 =42), 148.

Q74 Answer 99
Explanation: 120 (– 21), 99 (– 22), 77 (– 23), 54.

Q75 Answer 25
Explanation: to 35 add 11 = 46, then add 12 = 58, so subtract 10 from 35 to get 25.

Q76 Answer 60
Explanation: 60 (+ 7x1=7), 67 (+ 7x2=14), 81 (+ 7x3=21), 102 (+ 7x4=28), 130.

Q77 Answer 4
Explanation: the previous number is doubled each step.

Q78 Answer 48
Explanation: subtract 6 each step starting with 9x6=54.

Q79 Answer 5
Explanation: multiply the previous number by 5 each step starting with 1x5=5.

Q80 Answer 76
Explanation: 75(+ 1), 76 (+ 2), 78 (+ 3), 81.

Q81 Answer 0
Explanation: 3 (– 2), 1 (– 1), 0 (– 0), 0.

Q82 Answer 15
Explanation: 3 is added to the previous number each step, starting with 3x4=12.

Q83 Answer 100
Explanation: each number is half the previous number.

Q84 Answer 24
Explanation: subtract 12 from the previous step beginning with 4x12=48.

Q85 Answer 7
Explanation: multiply the previous number by 7 each step, 1x7 =7, 7x7= 49, 49x7=343.

Q86 Answer 106
Explanation: 71 (+17), 88 (+18), 106 (+19), 125.

Q87 Answer 111
Explanation: 120 (– 1x9=9), 111 (– 2x9=18), 93 (– 3x9=27), 66 (– 4x9=36), 30.

Q88 Answer 60
Explanation: 5 is added to the previous number each step starting with 5x10=50.

Q89 Answer 30
Explanation: add 6 to the previous number each step.

Q90 Answer 52
Explanation: 89 (– 19), 70 (– 18), 52 (– 17), 35.

Q91 Answer 66
Explanation: 66 (– 6x1=6), 60 (– 6x2=12) ,48 (– 6x3=18), 30 (– 6x4=24), 6.

Q92 Answer 11
Explanation: these are the factors of 22: 1x22, 2x11, 11x2, 22x1.

Q93 Answer 10100
Explanation: multiply the previous number by 10 each step, starting with 101 x 10 = 1010.

Q94 Answer 110
Explanation: 110 (+10), 120 (+11), 131 (+12), 143.

Q95 Answer 17
Explanation: subtract 7 from the previous number each step.

Q96 Answer 72
Explanation: 72 (– 2x9=18), 54 (– 2x10=20), 34 (– 2x11=22), 12.

Q97 Answer 3
Explanation: these are the factors of 12: 1x12, 2x6, 3x4, 4x3, 6x2, 12x1.

Q98 Answer 90
Explanation: subtract 9 from the previous number each step of the series, beginning with 12x9=108.

Q99 Answer 4

Explanation: multiply the previous number by 4 each step.

Q100 Answer 22

Explanation: 13 (+9), 22 (+10), 32 (+11), 43.

Q101 Answer –40

Explanation: subtract 40 from the previous number each step.

Q102 Answer 113

Explanation: 137 (– 24), 113 (– 25), 88 (– 26), 62.

Q103 Answer 11

Explanation: this is a part of the sequence of prime numbers. It is worth learning them: 5, 7, 11, 13, 17, 19, 23, 29, 31, 37, 41...

Q104 Answer 296

Explanation: 296 (– 8x12=96), 200 (– 7x12=84), 116 (– 6x12=72), 44 (– 5x12=60), –16.

Q105 Answer 35

Explanation: 8 (+8), 16 (+9), 25 (+10), 35.

Q106 Answer 7

Explanation: subtract 7 from the previous number at each step in the series.

Q107 Answer 45

Explanation: add 9 to the previous number at each step.

Q108 Answer 60

Explanation: subtract 15 from the previous number at each step.

Q109 Answer 42

Explanation: 108 (– 1x11=11), 97 (– 2x11=22), 75 (– 3x11=33), 42 (– 4x11=44), –2.

Q110 Answer 72
Explanation: 12 is added to the previous number at each step of the series, starting with 12x5=60.

Q111 Answer 268
Explanation: 312 (– 44), 268 (– 45), 223 (– 46), 177.

Q112 Answer 120
Explanation: 132 (– 1x12=12), 120 (– 2x12=24), 96 (– 3x12=36), 60 (– 4x12=48), 12.

Q113 Answer 33
Explanation: 3 is added to the previous number each step of the series, beginning with 3x9=27.

Q114 Answer B
Explanation: it is worth learning this very common sequence. 1x1x1 = 1, 2x2x2 = 8, 3x3x3 = 27, 4x4x4 = 64, 5x5x5 = 125.

Q115 Answer C
Explanation: prime numbers are whole numbers divisible only by 1 and themselves.

Q116 Answer A
Explanation: another sequence well worth remembering, this is the series of whole numbers multiplied by themselves: 1x1 = 2, 2x2 = 4, 3x3 = 9, 4x4 = 16, 5x5 = 25.

Q117 Answer 0
Explanation: 123 (– 40), 83 (– 41), 42 (– 42), 0.

Q118 Answer 1
Explanation: 61 (– 10x3=30), 31 (– 10x2=20), 11 (– 10x1=10), 1.

Q119 Answer 49

Explanation: this is the series of 7 raised to the powers 7^2, 7^3, 7^4, starting with 7, 7x7=49, 7x7x7=343.

Q120 Answer 36

Explanation: subtract 3 from the previous number at each step in the sequence, starting with 12x3=36.

Q121 Answer 9

Explanation: divide the previous number by 3 each step: 27÷3=9.

Q122 Answer 65

Explanation: 8 (+ 18), 26 (+ 19), 45 (+ 20), 65.

Q123 Answer 32

Explanation: 16 (+ 16), 32 (+ 17), 49 (+ 18), 67.

Q124 Answer 9

Explanation: these are the factors of 36. Missing is 9: 1x36, 2x18, 3x12, 4x9, 6x6, 9x4, 12x3, 18x2, 36x1.

Q125 Answer 49

Explanation: 78(– 15), 63(– 14), 49(– 13), 36.

Q126 Answer 45

Explanation: 93 (– 4x3=12), 81 (– 4x4=16), 65 (– 4x5=20), 45 (4x6=24), 21.

Q127 Answer 60

Explanation: subtract 6 from the previous number at each step of the series starting with 12x6=72.

Q128 Answer 34

Explanation: 21 (+ 6), 27 (+ 7), 34 (+ 8), 42.

Q129 Answer 48

Explanation: 8 is added to the previous number at each step beginning with 8x4=24.

Q130 Answer 31

Explanation: 31(– 6), 25(– 7), 18(– 8), 10.

Q131 Answer 100

Explanation: 100 (– 0x7=0), 100 (– 1x7=7), 93 (– 2x7 = 14), 79 (– 3x7=21), 58 (– 4x7=28), 30.

Q132 Answer 64

Explanation: this is a part of the series of cubed numbers beginning with 3x3x3=27, 4x4x4=64, 5x5x5=125, 6x6x6=216. It is one to try to remember.

Q133 Answer 46

Explanation: 46 (– 8), 38 (– 9), 29 (– 10), 19.

Q134 Answer 104

Explanation: 80 (+ 1x8=8), 88 (+ 2x8=16), 104 (+ 3x8=24), 128 (+ 4x8=32), 160.

Q135 Answer 67

Explanation: 7 (+ 19), 26 (+ 20), 46 (+ 21), 67.

Q136 Answer 129

Explanation: 30 (+ 2x11=22), 52 (+ 3x11=33), 85 (+ 4x11=44), 129 (+ 5x11=55), 184.

Q137 Answer 81

Explanation: This is the series of squared numbers beginning with 6x6=36, 7x7=49, 8x8=64, 9x9=81.

Q138 Answer 81

Explanation: 81 (+ 3), 84 (+ 4), 88 (+ 5), 93.

Q139 Answer 29

Explanation: 2 (+ 3x9=27), 29 (+ 4x9=36), 65 (+ 5x9=45), 110 (+ 6x9=54), 164.

Q140 Answer 260

Explanation: 330 (– 70), 260 (– 69), 191 (– 68), 123.

Q141 Answer 54

Explanation: 194(– 10x5=50), 144 (– 10x4=40), 104 (– 10x3=30), 74 (– 10x2=20), 54.

Q142 Answer 44

Explanation: 44 (+ 1x12=12), 56 (+ 2x12=24), 80 (+ 3x12=36), 116 (+ 4x12=48), 164.

Q143 Answer 64

Explanation: 3 (+ 30), 33 (+ 31), 64 (+ 32), 96.

Q144 Answer 18

Explanation: 6 is subtracted from the previous number at each step beginning with 6x5=30.

Q145 Answer 84

Explanation: 54 (+ 3x10=30), 84 (+ 4x10=40), 124 (+ 5x10=50), 174 (+ 6x10=60), 234.

Q146 Answer 2

Explanation: these are the factors of 14: 1x14, 2x7, 7x2, 14x1.

Q147 Answer 54

Explanation: 6 (+ 15), 21 (+ 16), 37 (+ 17), 54.

Q148 Answer 80

Explanation: 80 (+ 6x2=12), 92 (+ 6x3=18), 110 (– 6x4=24), 134 (+ 6x5=30), 164.

Q149 Answer 33
Explanation: subtract 3 from the previous number, beginning the sequence with 3x11=33.

Q150 Answer 67
Explanation: 19 (+ 7x2=14), 33 (+ 8x2=16), 49 (+ 9x2=18), 67 (+ 10x2=20), 87.

Q151 Answer 4
Explanation: these are the factors of 16: 1x16, 2x8, 4x4, 8x2, 16x1.

Q152 Answer 19
Explanation: 19 (– 3), 16 (– 2), 14 (– 1), 13.

Q153 Answer 10
Explanation: 10 (+ 1x12=12), 22 (+ 2x12=24), 46 (+ 3x12=36), 82 (+ 4x12=48), 130.

Q154 Answer 54
Explanation: 9 is added to the previous number, starting with 4x9=36.

Q155 Answer 83
Explanation: 60 (+ 11), 71 (+ 12), 83 (+ 13), 96.

Q156 Answer 36
Explanation: add 4 to the previous number at each step, starting with 4x7=28.

Q157 Answer19
Explanation: 19 (+ 3x1=3), 22 (+ 3x2=6), 28 (+ 3x3=9), 37 (+ 3x4=12), 49.

Q158 Answer 8
Explanation: this is the series of 8 raised by the powers 8^2, 8^3, 8^4.

Q159 Answer 70

Explanation: 70 (+ 10x5=50), 120 (+ 11x5=55), 175 (+ 12x5=60), 235 (+ 13x5=65), 300.

Q160 Answer 18

Explanation: 20 (– 2), 18 (– 1), 17 (– 0), 17.

Q161 Answer 61

Explanation: 41 (+ 20), 61 (+ 21), 82 (+ 22), 104.

Q162 Answer 1

Explanation: divide the previous number by 10 each step: 10÷10=1.

Q163 Answer 56

Explanation: subtract 8 from the previous number, starting with 8x10=80.

Q164 Answer 9

Explanation: these are the factors of 18: 1x18, 2x9, 3x6, 6x3, 9x2, 18x1.

Q165 Answer 138

Explanation: 54 (+ 7x12=84), 138 (+ 8x12=96), 234 (+ 9x12=108), 342 (+ 10x12=120), 462.

Q166 Answer 120

Explanation: 120 (+3), 123 (+4), 127 (+5), 132.

Q167 Answer 62

Explanation: 8 (+ 9x6=54), 62 (+ 10x6=60), 122 (+ 11x6=66), 188 (+ 12x6=72), 260.

Q168 Answer 36

Explanation: these are a part of the series of squared numbers beginning with the square of 4: 4x4=16, 5x5=25, 6x6=36, 7x7=49.

Q169 Answer 36
Explanation: 21 (+ 7), 28 (+ 8), 36 (+ 9), 45.

Q170 Answer 36
Explanation: subtract 9 from the previous number at each step in the series, starting with 6x9=54.

Q171 Answer 33
Explanation: 33 (+ 2x2=4), 37 (+ 2x3=6), 43 (+ 2x4=8), 51 (+ 2x5=10), 61.

Q172 Answer 125
Explanation: This is part of the series of cubed numbers beginning with 4x4x4=64, 5x5x5=125, 6x6x6= 216, 7x7x7=343. It is another one to remember.

Q173 Answer 22
Explanation: 55 (– 17), 38(– 16), 22 (– 15), 7.

Q174 Answer 192
Explanation: 72 (+ 4x8=32), 104 (+ 5x8=40), 144 (+ 6x8=48), 192 (+ 7x8=56), 248.

Q175 Answer 3
Explanation: 48 (– 16), 32 (– 15), 17 (– 14), 3.

Q176 Answer 104
Explanation: add 8 to the previous number at each step, beginning with 8x11=88.

Q177 Answer 9
Explanation: These are the factors of 27: 1x27, 3x9, 9x3, 27x1.

Q178 Answer 52
Explanation: 102 (–10x3=30), 72 (– 10x2=20), 52 (– 10x1=10), 42 (– 10x0=0), 42.

Q179 Answer 108

Explanation: 108 (– 4x7=28), 80 (– 4x8=32), 48 (– 4x9=36), 12.

Q180 Answer 121

Explanation: add 11 to the previous number each step starting with 11x11=110.

Q181 Answer 120

Explanation: 216(– 5x8=40), 176 (– 4x8=32), 144 (– 3x8=24), 120 (– 2x8=16), 104.

Q182 Answer 20

Explanation: 74 (– 19), 55 (– 18), 37(– 17), 20.

Q183 Answer 16

Explanation: these are the factors of 32: 1x32, 2x16, 4x8, 8x4, 16x2, 32x1.

Q184 Answer 30

Explanation: subtract 6 from the previous number in the series starting with 6x6=36.

Q185 Answer 216

Explanation: divide the previous number by 6 at each step: 1296÷6=216.

Q186 Answer 60

Explanation: 43 (+ 17), 60 (+ 18), 78 (+ 19), 97.

Q187 Answer 9

Explanation: add 9 to the previous number at each step starting with 9x1=9.

Q188 Answer 80
Explanation: 120 (– 5x8=40), 80 (– 5x9=45), 35 (– 5x10=50), –15 (– 5x11=55), –70.

Q189 Answer 60
Explanation: add 5 to the previous number starting with 5x12=60.

Q190 Answer 16
Explanation: 27 (– 5), 22 (– 6), 16 (– 7), 9.

Q191 Answer 145
Explanation: 288 (– 7x11=77), 211 (– 6x11=66), 145 (– 5x11=55), 90 (– 4x11=44), 46.

Q192 Answer 52
Explanation: add 4 to the previous number at each step starting with 4x11=44.

Q193 Answer 80
Explanation: 80 (– 26), 54 (– 25), 29 (– 24), 5.

Q194 Answer 20
Explanation: these are the factors of 20: 1x20, 2x10, 4x5, 5x4, 10x2, 20x1.

Q195 Answer 65
Explanation: 77 (– 4x3=12), 65 (– 5x3=15), 50 (– 6x3=18), 32.

Q196 Answer 99
Explanation: 99 (+ 30), 129 (+ 31), 160 (+ 32), 192.

Q197 Answer 60
Explanation: subtract 12 from the previous number at each step of the series starting with 7x12=84.

Q198 Answer 128
Explanation: the previous number is divided by 2 at each step in the series: 256÷2=128.

Q199 Answer 8
Explanation: divide the previous number by 25 at each step: 200÷25=8.

Q200 Answer 55
Explanation: 30 (+ 12), 42 (+ 13), 55 (+ 14), 69 (+ 15), 84.

Chapter 4

Forty questions that do *not* involve percentages but may require you to work fractions and ratios

Q1 Answer $5
Explanation: 1,000 ÷ 40 = 25, 1,800 ÷ 90 = 20, so individually they cost $5 less each if you buy the larger quantity.

Q2 Answer 120 litres
Explanation: 3 x 20 = 60, 15 x 4 = 60, 60 + 60 = 120.

Q3 Answer 390
Explanation: 13 x 30 = 390.

Q4 Answer 3,410
Explanation: if 13,700 applications are processed and 10,290 cards are issued then the remainder are declined. 13,700 – 10,290 = 3,410.

Q5 Answer 200
Explanation: 225 ÷ 9 = 25, so 25 responded positively leaving the rest as negative responses = 200.

Q6 Answer 4
Explanation: 36 pairs = 72 shoes, 72 ÷ 18 = 4.

Q7 Answer 1,000
Explanation: 85 ÷ 17 = 5 bottles per household, 5 x 200 = 1,000.

Q8 Answer 125 hours
Explanation: 30 minutes = 0.5 hour, 250 x 0.5 = 125.

Q9 Answer 19 hours
Explanation: 57 ÷ 3 = 19.

Q10 Answer 150
Explanation: you must add the two fractions but to do this you must first convert them to equivalents with the same denominator (bottom number): 1/3 = 4/12, 4/12 + 5/12 = 9/12. This allows you to conclude that 9/12 of 600 visited on the first two days and 3/12 visited on the remaining three days. 3/12 of 600 = 600/12 x 3 = 150.

Q11 Answer 15 kg
Explanation: 4050 ÷ 270 = 405 ÷ 27 (cancel zeros) =

$$\begin{array}{r} 15 \\ 27\overline{)405} \\ \underline{27} \\ 135 \end{array}$$

Q12 Answer 2,475 nautical miles
Explanation: you know 4/9 = 1,100. You must find 9/9: 1100 ÷ 4 = 275 x 9 = 2475. Do not forget the scale of nautical miles.

Q13 Answer 420
Explanation: this example underlines the importance of paying attention to detail as you must convert between pairs of shoes and individual shoes. 30 pairs = 60 shoes, 60 x 7 = 420.

Q14 Answer 4
Explanation: 228 ÷ 57 = 4.

Q15 Answer 180 g

Explanation: 270 ÷ 6 = 45, 45 x 4 = 180.

Q16 Answer 120

Explanation: 1/6 of the seats are unoccupied, 720 ÷ 6 = 120.

Q17 Answer 100

Explanation: you need to calculate the ratio 1:40 for the total of 20,000. 20,000 ÷ 40 = 500, so 500 cats are needed to realize the ratio of 1: 40, which is 100 more cats that there are currently.

Q18 Answer 80

Explanation: one hour = 60 minutes or 3600 seconds (60 x 60) ÷ 45 = 80. You might find it quicker to work with fractions: 45 seconds = 3/4 minute, so in 1 minute = 1 1/3 buses arrive, in 60 minutes = 60 + (1/3 of 60) 20 = 80 buses arrive.

Q19 Answer 5 hours and 36 minutes

Explanation: 7 hours = 7 x 60 = 420 minutes, 420 ÷ 5 = 84, so 84 minutes is spent on the internet. 420 – 84 = 336 minutes on other activities, 5 hours = 5 x 60 = 300 minutes. So the person spends 5 hours and 36 minutes on other activities.

Q20 Answer 510

Explanation: you must find 2/3 of 765: 765 ÷ 3 = 255 x 2 = 510.

Q21 Answer 364

Explanation: the family with young children uses 7 bottles of milk a week more, 7 x 52 = 364 bottles.

Q22 Answer 8

Explanation: 7 trips will carry a maximum of 147 delegates so there will need to be at least 8 trips.

Q23 Answer 18,000
Explanation: you must find 1/3 of 54,000. 54,000 ÷ 3 = 18,000.

Q24 Answer 1,350
Explanation: you must find 3/9 of 4050. 1+ 3 + 5 = 9, 4050 ÷ 9 = 450 x 3 = 1,350 blue T-shirts.

Q25 Answer 48
Explanation: you must divide the number of cans sold by 6. 288 ÷ 6 = 48.

Q26 Answer 3:5
Explanation: the total number of respondents is irrelevant to this question: all you need to do is reduce the ratio 210:350 to its simplest form. Cancel the zeros to give you 21:35, then your knowledge of the multiplication tables should tell you that 7 divides into both, giving you the ratio 3:5.

Q27 Answer 76,000
Explanation: you must add the three subtotals 34,640 + 19,750 + 21, 610 = 76,000.

Q28 Answer 600
Explanation: in a year the team must realize 1,800 sales to hit the target. By the end of the third quarter they have managed 1,200 leaving 600 to get in the last quarter. 12 x 150 = 1,800, 1,800 ÷ 4 = 450 per quarter.

Q29 Answer 42 kg
Explanation: 3.5 x 12 = 42.

Q30 Answer 15,120
Explanation: you need to calculate how many hours there are in a week and multiply that number by 90. The fact that the 90 hits were

an average means that you can ignore any concerns about busy and less busy times. 7 x 24 = 168 hours x 90 = 15,120.

Q31 Answer 50

Explanation: you must find out how many children attend each school on average when there are 12 and how many attend each school on average when there are 3 more schools. 3,000 ÷ 12 = 250 so each of the 12 schools would on average be attended by 250 children. The number of schools is increased to 15, 3,000 ÷ 15 = 200 so the decrease in the average number of children is from 250 to 200 = 50.

Q32 Answer 7,500

Explanation: you must calculate 3/7 of the total. 17,500 ÷ 7 = 2,500 x 3 = 7,500.

Q33 Answer 450

Explanation: you have to find the difference between 3/5 and 3/8 of 2,000. 3/5 x 2,000 = 1,200, 3/8 x 2,000 = 750, 1,200 – 750 = 450.

Q34 Answer 150

Explanation: you must work out how many items the machine can produce in one minute and then multiply this amount by 2 machines and 25 minutes. 180 ÷ 60 = 3. One machine then produces 3 items a minute. 3 x 2 = 6: the two machines will produce 6 items a minute. 6 x 25 = 150.

Q35 Answer 48

Explanation: divide 156 into the ratio 4:9. 4 + 9 = 13. 156 ÷ 13 = 12, 4 x 12 = 48.

Q36 Answer 81

Explanation: multiply 9 x 9 = 81.

Q37 Answer 90
Explanation: first subtract the number of children from the total. 4/5 of the guests are men, so 1/5 are women, so then find 1/5 of the remainder. 520 – 70 = 450 adult guests, 450 ÷ 5 = 90.

Q38 Answer 4.75 kg
Explanation: simply add the weights together: 1 + 1.5 + 0.75 + 0.5 + 1 = 4.75.

Q39 Answer 3,450 pairs
Explanation: each box holds 230 ÷2 = 115 pairs, 115 x 30 = 3,450.

Q40 Answer 5,175
Explanation: 115 x 3 = 345 x 15 = 5,175.

Introducing percentage number problems

Eighteen number problem questions that introduce the common types of percentage calculation

Percentages of quantities

Worked example

Q41 If a race occurs over 15 km and 25% of the distance remains, how many kilometres have the runners covered? Answer 11.25 km or 11,250 m.
Explanation: convert the percentage into a decimal (divide by 100) and multiply by the quantity. (Take care to convert the quantities into the appropriate unit as necessary.) In this instance you are required to calculate 75% and not 25% (which is the distance that remains). Divide 75 by 100 = 0.75 x 15 = 11.25 km.

Q42 Answer 4 hours 48 minutes
Explanation: 4 hours = 4 x 60 = 240 minutes. Convert 20% to its decimal equivalent 20 ÷ 100 = 0.20. To find the new journey time calculate 240 x 0.20 = 48, then add the original 240 = 288 minutes or 4 hours 48 minutes.

Q43 Answer 45 g
Explanation: you are required to identify 15% of 300: 15% ÷100 = 0.15, 300 x 0.15 = 45.

Percentage decrease

Worked example

Q44 If a currency is devalued from $100 to $97, what is this decrease expressed as a percentage? Answer 3%
Explanation: to calculate percentage decreases divide the amount of decrease by the original amount and multiply the answer by 100. In this example you have to find the percentage decrease from 100 to 97: 100 –97 = 3, 3 ÷ 100 = 0.03 x 100 = 3.

Q45 Answer 75%
Explanation: 1,000 – 250 = 750, 750 ÷100 = 0.75 x 100 = 75.

Q46 Answer 18%
Explanation: ignore the fact that the given values are percentages and do the percentage decrease calculation in the usual way. 10 – 8.2 = 1.8, 1.8 ÷ 10 = 0.18 x 100 = 18%.

Percentage increase

Worked example

Q47 If the number of insurance claims per 1,000 policies was to increase from 20 to 30, what is the percentage increase in claims? Answer 50%
Explanation: calculate the percentage increase: divide the increase by the original amount and then multiply the answer by 100. In this instance the increase = 10 ÷ 20 (the original sum) = 0.5 x 100 = 50%.

Q48 Answer 30%
Explanation: 910 – 700 = 210, 210 ÷ 700 = 0.3, 0.3 x 100 = 30.

Q49 Answer 40%
Explanation: 56 – 40 = 16, 16 ÷ 40 = 0.4, 0.4 x 100 = 40.

Percentage change

Worked example

Q50 If the list price of a commodity is adjusted by 0.3 to a new high value of 2.8, what is the percentage change in value? Answer 12% increase
Explanation: the adjustment leads to a new high: this means the change is an increase. We can calculate the previous price was 2.8 – 0.3 = 2.5. We now must calculate the percentage change between 2.5 and 2.8. 2.5 – 2.8 = 0.3, 0.3 ÷ 2.5 = 0.12 x 100 = 12.

Q51 Answer 5% decrease
Explanation: you must calculate the percentage decrease between 7 and 6.65 (a change of 0.35). Do this by dividing the decrease by the original amount, 0.35 ÷ 7 = 0.05 x 100 = 5%. Don't forget to say it is a decrease.

Q52 Answer 60% increase
Explanation: first calculate the higher price: 36 + 21.6 = 57.6. Now calculate the percentage increase (divide the increase by the original amount): 21.6 ÷ 36 = 0.6 x 100 = 60% increase.

One number expressed as a percentage of another

Worked example

Q53 50 people responded to a survey and 30 indicated that they had a passport. What percentage of the respondents said they held this document? Answer 60%
Explanation: a percentage is a fraction with a denominator of 100. To express one number as a percentage of another, express the numbers as fractions and then convert to an equivalent with a denominator of 100. In this instance you must convert 30/50 into an equivalent fraction ?/100. Do this by multiplying top and bottom by 2 = 60/100 = 60%.

Q54 Answer 25%

Explanation: you must convert 4/16 into a percentage: 4/16 = 1/4 = 25/100 = 25%.

Q55 Answer 20%

Explanation: you must convert 1/5 into a percentage: 1/5 = 20/100 = 20%.

Percentage profit and loss

Worked example

Q56 If you buy some high-yield stock at $10 and sell it at $14 what is the percentage profit or loss? Answer 40% profit

Explanation: to find the percentage profit divide the amount of profit by the buying price and multiply by 100. To find a percentage loss divide the loss by the buying price and multiply by 100. In this instance 14 – 10 = 4, so profit = 4, 4 ÷ 10 = 0.4 x 100 = 40%. Do not forget to say whether it is a profit or a loss.

Q57 Answer 20% loss

Explanation: 10 – 8 – 2, 2 ÷ 10 = 0.2 x 100 = 20.

Q58 Answer 25% profit

Explanation: 75 – 60 = 15, 15 ÷ 60 = 0.25 x 100 = 25%.

Forty-two more number problems

Q59 Answer 25%

Explanation: you have to express 4/16 as a percentage. 4/16 = 1/4 = 25/100= 25%.

Q60 Answer 40%

Explanation: you must find 2/5 as a percentage. 2/5 = 40/100 (multiply both by 20) = 40%.

Q61 Answer 15%
Explanation: you have to express 12/80 as a percentage. 12/80 = 3/20 (divide both by 4) then multiply both by 5 to make a fraction of 100 = 15/100 = 15%.

Q62 Answer 2% decrease
Explanation: 4.4 ÷ 220 = 0.02 x 100 = 2. Remember to state it is a decrease.

Q63 Answer 100,000 times larger
Explanation: if you multiply 5.3 x 100,000 you get 530,000. You do this by moving the decimal point 5 places to the left. 5 decimal places = 100,000 (5 zeros).

Q64 Answer 12.5
Explanation: first find out the number of brown eggs then calculate the percentage. 1/3 of 72 = 72 ÷ 3 = 24, so 24 eggs were brown. Now express 3/24 as a percentage. 3/24 cancels to 1/8, 100 ÷ 8 = 12.5.

Q65 Answer 0.25%
Explanation: you must find 0.2 of 80. 0.2/80 = 2/800 = 1/400 = 0.25/100 = 0.25%.

Q66 Answer 40%
Explanation: 60 – 36 = 24 seconds, the time saved. You have to find 24 as a percentage of 60. 24/60 = 2/5 (highest common factor (HCF) =12) = 40/100 = 40%.

Q67 Answer 3 hours and 19 minutes
Explanation: approach this sort of question in stages. 10.21–11.00 = 39 minutes, 11.00–14.00 = 3 hours, 14.00–14.40 = 40 minutes. Now add the bits up: 39 minutes + 40 minutes = 79 minutes = 1 hour 19 minutes, + 3 hours = 4 hours and 19 minutes. Finally, deduct the one-hour break = 3 hours and 19 minutes.

Q68 Answer 10% increase

Explanation: this is an easy question hidden among possibly confusing detail. The size of the team and the number of days on which they exceed the target are irrelevant details to the question. You simply need to calculate the percentage change between 2,400 and 2,640. 2,640 – 2,400 = 240. 240 ÷ 2,400 = 0.10 x 100 = 10% Remember to identify it as an increase.

Q69 Answer 12 km

Explanation: 18 ÷ 60 (minutes in an hour) = 0.3 km. This is how far the cyclist can travel in one minute, so for 40 minutes multiply 0.3 x 40 = 12.

Q70 Answer 30% profit

Explanation: gross means before the deduction of certain costs, for example tax or depreciation, but you can ignore this detail and focus on the calculation, which requires you to work out the percentage profit. 750 = profit, 750 ÷ 2,500 = 0.3 x 100 = 30% profit.

Q71 Answer $13,800

Explanation: the car is sold at 92% of the list price (100 – 8 = 92) so you must calculate 92% of 15,000. 92 as a decimal = 0.92, 15,000 x 0.92 = 13,800.

Q72 Answer 110%

Explanation: if you gave the answer as 10% then you mistakenly calculated the percentage increase when the question required you to calculate 3.3 as a percentage of 3. 33/30 = 1 and 3/30 = 1 and 1/10 = 100% + 1/10 = 100% +10% = 110%.

Q73 Answer 80%

Explanation: calculate this year's crop 12.5 – 2.5 = 10, then you must find 10 as a percentage of 12.5. 10/12.5 get rid of the decimal by multiplying top and bottom by 10 = 100/125, which cancels to 4/5 = 80/100 = 80%.

Q74 Answer 5%
Explanation: because we are talking about the minutes in an hour this is a different sum from the percentage change between 45 and 48. 48 – 45 = 3, so you must find 3 as a percentage of 60. 3/60 = 1/20 = 5%.

Q75 Answer 80%
Explanation: 12 – 2.4 = 9.6 loss, 9.6 ÷ 12 = 0.8, 0.8 x 100 = 80.

Q76 Answer 15%
Explanation: of the 50 surveyed only 40 answered so you must find 6 as a percentage of 40. 6/40 = 3/20 = 15/100 = 15%.

Q77 Answer 6,480
Explanation: you have to calculate how many shares they currently hold and subtract this from 51% of 48,000. Add 1/8 + 1/4 (first convert 1/4 to its equivalent 2/8) = 3/8, 3/8 x 48,000 (6x8= 48) so 1/8 = 6,000 x 3 = 18,000, the number of shares they currently hold, 51% x 48,000 = 48,000/100 x 51. Cancel the zeros = 480 x 51 = 24,480, the number they need to have a controlling interest. 24,480 – 18,000 = 6,480, the number of further shares they need.

Q78 Answer All of it is completed
Explanation: a bit of a trick question. You have to add 6/15 and 3/5. Do this by converting the fractions to equivalents with the same denominator: in this case 3/5 = 9/15, 6/15 + 9/15 = 15/15 = 1 so the project is completed.

Q79 Answer 12.5%
Explanation: you must find 62.5 as a percentage of 500. 62.5/500 (divide both top and bottom by 5) = 12.5/100 = 12.5%.

Q80 Answer 20
Explanation: 4 + 2 + 1 = 7, divide 35 by 7 = 5, to make 35 litres at the ratio of 4:2:1 you will therefore need 20 : 10 : 5 litres of each ingredient.

Q81 Answer 5%
Explanation: 6,000 – 5,700 = 300 late letters. So you must find 300 as a percentage of 6,000. 300/6,000 = 3/60 = 1/20 = 5/100 = 5%.

Q82 Answer 6% loss
Explanation: 650 – 611 = 39, 39 ÷ 650 = 0.06 x 100 = 6.

Q83 Answer 3 hours and 36 minutes
Explanation: you must find 1/5 of the journey time and add it to the expected journey time, 3 hours = 180 minutes ÷ 5 = 36 minutes, add the 3 hours = 3 hours and 36 minutes.

Q84 Answer 25%
Explanation: to answer this first find the previous year's profit, then add 15,000 and calculate the new total as a percentage of 500,000. 22% of 500,000 = 22/100 x 500,000, cancel the zeros to get 22 x 5,000 = 110,000. Add 15,000 = 125,000. Now calculate 125,000 as a percentage of 500,000. 125,000/500,000 cancel zeros to get 125/500, divide top and bottom by 5 = 25%.

Q85 Answer 40%
Explanation: 0.7 – 0.5 = 0.2. You must find 0.2 as a percentage increase from 0.5. 0.2 ÷ 0.5 = 0.4 x 100 = 40%.

Q86 Answer 30% drop
Explanation: 70 – 49 = 21, 21 ÷ 70 = 0.3 x 100 = 30% drop.

Q87 Answer 9 seconds sooner
Explanation: you have to identify 3% of 5 minutes. 5 minutes = 60 x 5 seconds = 300 seconds, 3% of 300 = 9.

Q88 Answer 30%
Explanation: you must identify 1.5/5 as a percentage, 1.5/5 = 3/10 and 3/10 is = to 30%.

Q89 Answer 2,200
Explanation: approach this in stages. First convert the ratio to a fraction, then add the fractions and then calculate the number of staff that remain. To convert the ratio simply place the first number above the second 1: 8 = 1/8, to add 1/8 + 3/16 convert 1/8 to the equivalent 2/16, 2/16 + 3/16 = 5/16. You cannot work out that 11/16 of the workforce remains. 11/16 x 3,200 = 3,200 ÷ 16 = 200 x 11 = 2,200.

Q90 Answer 20% reduction
Explanation: you must find the percentage decrease between 40 and 32. 40 – 32 = 8, 8 ÷ 40 = 0.2 x 100 = 20.

Q91 Answer 75% loss
Explanation: 28,000 – 7,000 = 21,000 loss, 21,000 ÷ 28,000 = cancel the zeros 21 ÷ 28 = 0.75 x 100 = 75%.

Q92 Answer 10
Explanation: 100 items x 10 packs = 1,000 items in each box, 1,000 x 100 = 100,000 items in each truck so you need 10 trucks to carry one million items. 100,000 x 10 = one million.

Q93 Answer 15%
Explanation: total revenue = 36,000 + 204,000 = 240,000. You must find 36,000 as a percentage of 240,000. Cancel zeros to give 36 as a percentage of 240 = 36/240, divide both top and bottom by 12 = 3/20 = 15/100 = 15%.

Q94 Answer 22% profit
Explanation: first you must calculate the profit = income – operating costs = 12,000 – 9,360 = 2,640 profit. Now find 2,640 as a percentage of 12,000: 2,640 ÷ 12,000 = 0.22 x 100 = 22%.

Q95 Answer 603

Explanation: you must calculate the number of seats in total minus the number of unoccupied seats and add the number of people standing. 8 x 72 = 576 seats – 13 unoccupied = 563, 563 + 40 people standing = 603.

Q96 Answer 1.2% profit

Explanation: first calculate total turnover and total profit. Total turnover is 150,000 + 850,000 = 1,000,000. Total profit = 15,000 – 3,000 = 12,000. So overall percentage profit = 12,000. As a percentage of 1,000,000 cancel zeros to get 12 as a percentage of 1,000 = 1.2%.

Q97 Answer 30%

Explanation: first establish the capacity of container B and then calculate the percentage of the total. 22 – 15.4 = 6.6 (the capacity of B). Now calculate 6.6 as a percentage of 22: 6.6/22 = 66/220 (HCF 11); 6/20 = 30/100 = 30%.

Q98 Answer $15,000

Explanation: you need to calculate 2% and 4.5% of 600,000: the difference between these amounts is the answer. 2% = 2/100 x 600,000; cancel zeros to get 2 x 6,000 = 12,000. 4.5% = 4.5/100 x 600,000; cancel zeros to get 4.5 x 6,000 = 27,000. 27,000 – 12,000 = 15,000.

Q99 Answer 6 hours and 42 minutes

Explanation: make the calculation as a series of convenient steps. 13.25–14.00 = 35 minutes, 14.00–20.00 = 6 hours, 20.00–20.07 = 7 minutes. Add these three subtotals together = 6 hours and 42 minutes.

Q100 Answer 25%

Explanation: start by calculating the profit and turnover for the product and then perform the percentage calculation. 1/2 of 6,000 = 3,000 profit. 1/10 of 120,000 = 12,000 turnover. Now calculate 3,000 as a percentage of 12,000. Cancel zeros to get 3 as a percentage of 12 = 3/12 = 1/4 = 25%.

Chapter 5

A hundred practice questions

Q1 Answer 30

Explanation: the total for all four products is given as 90. Add the three given quantities and subtract them from 90 to get the value for quantity 1: 15 + 25 +20 = 60, 90 – 60 = 30.

Q2 Answer 120°

Explanation: the total number of degrees = 360 and the total quantity is 90. For each item we must allow 90/360 = 4°. 30 x 4 = 120°.

Q3 Answer 60°

Explanation: 15 x 4 = 60. Don't forget the degree sign = 60°.

Q4 Answer 100°

Explanation: 25 x 4 = 100.

Q5 Answer 80°

Explanation: 20 x 4 = 80.

Employment by industry

Q6 Answer 12,240,000 or 12.24 million

Explanation: add the two values to get the total. Remember to state the value in millions.

Q7 Answer 11%

Explanation: you must find 2.64 as a percentage of 24. 2.64/24 = 0.11 x 100 = 11%.

Q8 Answer 35%

Explanation: you must find 7.7 as a percentage of 22. 7.7 ÷ 22 = 0.35 x 100 = 35%.

Q9 Answer 56%

Explanation: you must combine the service and manufacturing subtotals. Calculate this as a percentage of all employment, and give the balance from 100% as the answer. 7.7 + 1.98 = 9.68, 9.68 as a percentage of 22 = 9.68 ÷ 22 = 0.44 x 100 = 44%, 100 – 44 = 56.

Q10 Answer Decrease

Explanation: between 2000 and 2005 all employment increased by 2 million. During the same period the workforces of the service and manufacturing sectors increased by 2.56 million. Other sectors must therefore have suffered a decrease in their share of total employment.

Sales volumes of old and new designs

Q11 Answer B

Explanation: the sales figures given on the table can be compared with the line graph and used to identify B as the line representing sales for the old design.

Q12 Answer The shaded bar

Explanation: the value can be taken from the table and used to correctly identify the shaded bar.

Q13 Answer 1,250

Explanation: this information can be read off the line graph.

Q14 Answer X
Explanation: the lines on which we plot numbers on a graph are called axes. Usually the horizontal line is called the x axis and the vertical line the y axis.

Sales by region from table to pie graph

Q15 Answer Region 3
Explanation: first calculate the sales for the missing region by subtracting the subtotals for regions 1,2 and 4 from the total, then you can identify region 3 as having the highest number of sales. 250 + 500 + 125 = 875, 1,500 – 875 = 625.

Q16 Answer 60°
Explanation: you know from the total that segment 1 represents 250/1,500 so you must calculate 250/1,500 x 360 = 1/6 x 360 = 60.

Q17 Answer 33%
Explanation: you must calculate 500 as a percentage of 1,500 = 500/1,500 = 1/3 = $0.3\dot{3}$ x 100 = 33%.

Q18 Answer 120°
Explanation: segment 2 represents 500/1,500 so calculate 500/1,500 x 360 = 1/3 x 360 = 120.

Q19 Answer 1/12
Explanation: you must express in its simplest form 125 as a fraction of 1,500. 125/1,500 = 1/12 (HCF 12).

Q20 Answer 150°
Explanation: you have already worked out that region 3 has sales of 625. Now calculate 625/1,500 x 360, 625/1,500 = 5/12 (HCF12). 5/12 x 360 = 150°.

Analysis of a workforce by grade and gender

Q21 Answer 250

Explanation: find 12% of 1,750 and 4% of 1,000 and add these two figures together. 12/100 x 1,750 = 0.12 x 1,750 = 210, 4/100 x 1,000 = 0.4 x 1,000 = 40, 210 + 40 = 250.

Q22 Answer 390

Explanation: you must find 39% of 1,000, 39/100 x 1,000 = 0.39 x 1,000 = 390.

Q23 Answer Women

Explanation: you must establish which is largest, 30% of 1,750 or 57% of 1,000. 30/100 x 1,750 = 0.3 x 1,750 = 525 men, 57/100 x 1,000 = 0.57 x 1,000 = 570, so the answer is women.

Q24 Answer 84%

Explanation: you previously calculated that the number of management positions = 250 and that 210 were filled by men. Now calculate 210 as a percentage of 250 to find the percentage of men in these grades. 210/250 x 100 = 84.

Q25 Answer 1 : 10

Explanation: you have previously calculated that 250 people work in management positions, total jobs = 2,750 – 250, so 2,500 people work in non-managerial positions. You must express the ratio 250 : 2,500 in its simplest form: divide both by 250 = 1 : 10.

Monthly average expenditure for a fictitious household

Q26 Answer Yes

Explanation: add together 30 + 7 + 15 = 52, so 52% of the expenditure goes on these items which is more than half.

Q27 Answer 72°
Explanation: you have to find 20% of 360 to find the angle of the segment. Do this quickly by working out 10% and doubling it, 360 x 10% = 36 x 2 = 72.

Q28 Answer Cannot tell
Explanation: a bit of a trick question but one that underlines the importance of attention to detail. You cannot tell how much of the family's income is spent on these items because no information is given regarding income. The information only relates to expenditure.

Q29 Answer $60,000
Explanation: you must calculate 100% when 7% = 350 and multiply by 12 for the annual figure. 350 = 7% so 350/7 = 1% = 50, 50 x 100 = 100% = 5,000 x 12 = 60,000.

Q30 Answer $120
Explanation: you must divide 180 into the ratio 2:1:6 and give the share for gifts, 2 + 1 + 6 = 9, 180/9 = 20 x 6 = 120.

Extracts from the accounts of struggling.com

Q31 Answer False
Explanation: sales in 2002 were 900,000. For the statement to be true sales in 2003 would need to be 110% of this figure. 110% of 900,000 = 900,000 + 90,000 = 990,000 but sales in 2003 were 910,000 so the statement is false.

Q32 Answer $930,000
Explanation: the gross profit/loss position carried forward went from 10,000 profit in 2001 to 20,000 loss in 2002, a 30,000 adverse change, so expenses in 2002 must have been 30,000 more than sales. 900,000 + 30,000 = 930,000 – don't forget the $ sign.

Q33 Answer $40,000

Explanation: find the gross profit by subtracting the year's expenses from sales: 910 – 870 = 40. Remember the zeros for 000s and the $ sign.

Q34 Answer Cannot tell

Explanation: sales can be calculated by adding gross profits to expenses but the gross profit is not given, only the gross profit carried forward. This means that the 10,000 profit may not relate to 2001 but could be a figure carried forward from the previous year, so the calculation cannot be done and we cannot tell if the statement is true or false.

Q35 Answer True

Explanation: you have already calculated that the gross loss for 2002 was 30,000. You can calculate that the profit for 2003 was 40,000 (910,000 – 870,000) so you can tell that it is true that the gross profit figure for 2003 was 70,000 better than the 2002 figure.

Analysis of contributions to overall gross profit by ore/commodity

Q36 Answer 1 thousand million

Explanation: the scale of the graph shows for example 184 m as just under 2/10 of 1 bn so 1 bn is taken as 1 thousand million in this instance. Both definitions are in use but this one is more commonly used.

Q37 Answer $2.2 bn

Explanation: add the four figures to get the total (but take care when adding billions and millions) 0.9 + 1.05 + 0.184 + 0.066 = 2.2. Note 66 million = 0.066 bn.

Q38 Answer Cannot tell
Explanation: the graph shows gross profit but no information is given for the value of sales so you cannot tell if the statement is true or false.

Q39 Answer True
Explanation: half of the gross profit = 1/2 x 2.2 bn = 1.1 bn. Add the gross profits of copper and aluminium = 1.05 bn + 66 m = 1.16 bn which is just over 1.1, so the statement is true.

Q40 Answer $0.75 bn
Explanation: the total gross profit was calculated in a previous question as 2.2 bn. You must subtract 2.95 – 2.2 = 0.75.

Market share

Q41 Answer 200 m
Explanation: you know that 56% = 112 m, and you must find 100%. Calculate 112 ÷ 56 x 100 = 2 x 100 = 200.

Q42 Answer 8 : 1
Explanation: Market Leader holds 56% of the market compared with Others 7%, so you must express the ratio 56 : 7 in its simplest form. 7 x 8 = 56 so 56 : 7 = 8 : 1.

Q43 Answer x 4 or 4 times bigger
Explanation: Small Player has a 5% share compared with Competitor's 20%. 20 ÷ 5 = 4, so Competitor's share is 4 times bigger.

Q44 Answer x3 or 3 times bigger
Explanation: 1/2 of Competitor's share = 20 ÷ 2 = 10. This means that Small Player's share would increase from 5% to 15%, a threefold increase.

Q45 Answer $225 m

Explanation: 12% = 27 m; you must find 100%. 27 ÷ 12 = 1%. 27 ÷ 12 x 100 = 100%. 27 ÷ 12 = 2.25 x 100 = 225.

Scale of production and unit cost

Q46 Answer $150,000

Explanation: fixed costs = total costs – variable costs: 230 – 80 = 150. Don't forget the $ and the zeros to signify thousands.

Q47 Answer $157,000

Explanation: variable costs = total costs – fixed costs: 307 – 150 = 157.

Q48 Answer $375,000

Explanation: total costs = fixed costs + variable costs: 150 + 225 = 375.

Q49 Answer $11,500

Explanation: unit cost = 460,000 ÷ 40 = 11,500.

Q50 Answer $1,100

Explanation: first calculate the unit cost for 50 units and then subtract it from the unit cost for 40 units (which you calculated for the last question). 50 units = 520,000 ÷ 50 = 10,400, 11,500 – 10,400 = $1,100.

Labour and capital productivity

Q51 Answer 26,250

Explanation: labour productivity x labour hours = output, so 30 x 875 = 26,250.

Q52 Answer 5

Explanation: output ÷ capital productivity = number of machines = 26,250 ÷ 5,250 = 5.

Q53 Answer 32
Explanation: labour productivity = 29,600 ÷ 925 = 32.

Q54 Answer 1,000
Explanation: labour hours = output ÷ labour productivity = 34,500 ÷ 34.5 = 1,000.

Q55 Answer 6,900
Explanation: capital productivity = 34,500 ÷ 5 = 6,900.

Capacity utilization

Q56 Answer 520,000
Explanation: the maximum production is the sum of 250,000 + 150,000 + 120,000 = 520,000.

Q57 Answer 36,000
Explanation: the maximum production for product C is 120,000 and actual production = 84,000 so spare capacity = 120,000 – 84,000 = 36,000.

Q58 Answer 90%
Explanation: make the sum more convenient by cancelling the zeros, then you must find 225 as a percentage of 250: 225/250 (divide both by 25) 9/10 x 100 = 90%.

Q59 Answer 80%
Explanation: 120/150 = 0.8 x 100 = 80%.

Q60 Answer Decrease
Explanation: the more capacity is utilized the greater the actual output for a given level of fixed cost; you would therefore expect the cost per unit to decrease the more that capacity is utilized.

Profit and loss

Q61 Answer $74,800

Explanation: gross profit = sales turnover – cost of sales = 110 – 35.2 = 74.8. Remember the $ sign and the zeros.

Q62 Answer $37,400

Explanation: net profit = sales turnover – cost of sales – overheads = 110 – 35.2 – 37.4 =37.4. That is, $37,400.

Q63 Answer $7,480

Explanation: you must find 20% of 37,400. You can do this quickly by calculating 10% and doubling it, 20% of 37,400 = 3,740 x 2 = 7,480.

Q64 Answer $19,920

Explanation: retained profit = net profit – tax and dividend = 37,400 – 7,480 – 10,000 = 19,920.

Q65 Answer 68%

Explanation: to find the percentage gross profit you must calculate gross profit ÷ sales turnover x 100. 74.8/110 x 100 = 0.68 x 100 = 68%.

Budgets verses actual

Q66 Answer 80%

Explanation: budgeted revenue was 250 (000) actual was 200 (000) so calculate 200 as a percentage of 250 to find the percentage realized. 200/250 x 100 = 4/5 x 100 = 80.

Q67 Answer 12%

Explanation: the budget for material costs was 125, while the actual was 110. The actual was then 15 below budget. You must calculate 15 as a percentage of 125 = 15/125 x 100 = 3/25 x 100 = 12%.

Q68 Answer $20,000
Explanation: subtract the material and labour costs from the revenue (all figures actual) to get the actual net profit = 200 – 110 – 70 = 20, remember the $ sign and 000s.

Q69 Answer 20%
Explanation: the revenue would increase to 225 and the net profit to 45. So you must find 45 as a percentage of 225 = 45/225 x 100 = 1/5 x 100 = 20.

Q70 Answer 40%
Explanation: you must calculate 20 (the actual) as a percentage of 50 (the budgeted net profit). 20/50 x 100 = 2/5 x 100 = 40%.

Cash flow

Q71 Answer $1.93 m
Explanation: it can be seen from Period 1 that total cash is obtained by adding opening balance to sale receipts and collection from aged debt. So total cash for period 2 = 0.13 + 1.5 + 0.3 = 1.93.

Q72 Answer $2.15 m
Explanation: the calculation of total outgoings can be established from Period 1. Add tax, wages net, materials and other cost outgoings = total outgoings = 0.43 + 0.62 + 1.0 + 0.1 = 2.15.

Q73 Answer $0.28 m or $280,000
Explanation: the closing balance is total cash – total outgoings for the period = 1.93 – 1.65 = $0.28 m.

Q74 Answer None or zero
Explanation: the total outgoings for period 2 were 1.65 and this is fully accounted for when you total net wages, materials and other cash outgoings for that period, so no tax was paid.

Q75 Answer $1.98 m

Explanation: sales receipts + collection = 1.65 + 0.33 = $1.98 m.

Employment for the month of December 2005

Q76 Answer +39,000

Explanation: the net total means the total when you balance all the pluses and minuses depending on the industry. So add and subtract the pluses and minuses to get a total (6 +98 +3) = 107 (– 20 – 48) = 39. Remember the 000s and the fact it is positive = +39,000.

Q77 Answer 900

Explanation: total the losses and subtract this subtotal from 9,200 to identify the job losses in the South West region. 2,000 + 1,900 + 1,100 + 2,600 + 700 = 8,300, 9,200 – 8,300 = 900.

Q78 Answer South and North East

Explanation: 50% of the total = 9,200 ÷ 2 = 4,600. Only the subtotals for South and North East total this amount.

Q79 Answer –157,000

Explanation: don't try to modify your previous calculation. The safest approach is to redo the calculation from scratch. (–98 + –20 + –48) = –166 + (6 + 3) = 157. Remember the $000s.

Q80 Answer False

Explanation: the figure for the region with the second lowest total is not given on the table but it was the South West with 900. The North was the third lowest.

Frequency of jobs by sector advertised over a five day period

Q81 Answer 360
Explanation: you must add the positions = 144 + 36 + 126 + 54 = 360.

Q82 Answer 15%
Explanation: you must express 54 as a percentage of 360. 360% = 3.6, 54 ÷ 3.6 = 15.

Q83 Answer False
Explanation: the same number of jobs were advertised in these two sectors. Public and professional = 180, hotel and catering and retail and distribution = 180 also.

Q84 Answer 40%
Explanation: you must express 144 as a percentage of 360. 3.6 = 1%, 144 ÷ 3.6 = 40.

Q85 Answer 36°
Explanation: all jobs = 360 therefore each job = 1°. Therefore the angle for the 36 professional positions would equal 36°.

A disappointing summer

Q86 Answer Region 1
Explanation: Region 1 experienced 306 hours.

Q87 Answer 280 hours
Explanation: you must find 100% when you know 210 = –25%, 210 therefore must equal 75%. Find 100% by calculating 210 ÷ 75 x 100 = 2.8 x 100 = 280.

Q88 Answer 60%

Explanation: Region 4 experienced –40% so 222 hours = 60% of the average.

Q89 Answer Region 4

Explanation: to identify which is higher you must calculate the average number of hours for each of the two regions. Region 1 306 hours = 85% so calculate 100%: 306 ÷ 85 = 3.6 x 100 = 360 hours. Region 4 222 hours = 60%, so 222 ÷ 60 x 100 = 100%, 222 ÷ 60 = 3.7 x 100 = 370 hours. So historically Region 4 enjoys the higher average level of sunshine.

Q90 Answer 6 hours

Explanation: you know from the table that 294 = 100 – 2 = 98% of the average. You must find the value of 2%. 294 ÷ 98 = 1%, 294 ÷ 98 x 2 = 2%, 294 x 98 = 3 x 2 = 6 hours.

Number of people celebrating their 100th birthday

Q91 Answer True

Explanation: over the two years illustrated the total for the three countries is 159 people.

Q92 Answer Cannot tell

Explanation: more people in France celebrated their 100th birthday but you cannot infer from this that people live longer in that country.

Q93 Answer 12%

Explanation: you must find the percentage increase between 75 and 84, an increase of 9. Find this by dividing the increase by the original amount and multiplying by 100. 9/75 = 0.12 x 100 = 12.

Q94 Answer False
Explanation: in France 90 people celebrated their 100th birthday. For the statement to be true 45 in Italy would have celebrated 100 years. In fact 48 people in Italy did, so the statement is false.

Q95 Answer True
Explanation: 15 Germans celebrated in 2004; this figure dropped to 6 in 2005, a fall of 9. To test the statement you must see if 60% of 15 = 9. 15 x 60 ÷ 100 = 9, so the statement is true.

The balance of power

Q96 Answer 30%
Explanation: you have to express 54 as a percentage of **180. 54/180** x 100 = 3/10 x 100 =30%.

Q97 Answer Christian Democrats and Socialist Coalition
Explanation: you must find half of 135 = 67.5. This means that a majority would be 68 or more seats. The only two parties that would secure a majority if they formed an alliance are the Christian Democrats (41 seats) and the Socialist Coalition (27 seats) = 68 seats.

Q98 Answer 159
Explanation: 68 in the lower house and (180 ÷ 2) + 1 = 91 in the upper, 68 + 91 = 159.

Q99 Answer 45%
Explanation: you must add the total seats held by the three parties and express this as a percentage of 180. The three parties hold 29 + 25 + 27 = 81 seats, 81/180 x 100 = their shared percentage of all seats in the upper house, 81/180 x 100 = 9/20 x 100 = 45.

Q100 Answer 105

Explanation: you must add together the number of seats in both houses and then divide that total by 3 to find 1/3. 180 + 135 = 315 ÷ 3 = 105.

Chapter 6

Test 1 Number problems

Q1 Answer 78%

Explanation: 80.1 – 45 = 35.1, 35.1 ÷ 45 = 0.78 x 100 = 78%.

Q2 Answer 33%

Explanation: first find the day-time temperature = 0.6 + 1.2 = 1.8. Now find 0.6 as a percentage of 1.8: 0.6/1.8 = 6/18 = 1/3 = 33/100 = 33%.

Q3 Answer Decrease

Explanation: first calculate the assumed percentage of claims and then establish if it is an increase or decrease. 300 as a percentage of 2,500 = 300/2,500. Cancel zeros = 3/25. Multiply top and bottom by 4 = 12/100 = 12%. You can now see that the actual number of claims was less than the assumed level so it was a decrease.

Q4 Answer 300%

Explanation: first work out the difference between the winter and summer, then calculate the percentage increase. 20 – 5 = 15, now calculate 15 ÷ 5 = 3, 3 x 100% = 300 = 300%.

Q5 Answer 3 hours and 3 minutes

Explanation: calculate each stage separately. 7.42 to 8.00 = 18 minutes, 8.00–9.00 = 1 hour, add one hour and 5 minutes to 9.00 = 10.05, 10.05–11.00 = 55 minutes, 11.00–11.50 = 50 minutes. Now add the minutes: 18 + 55 + 50 = 123 = 2 hours and 3 minutes. Don't forget the 1 hour between 8.00 and 9.00 = 3 hours and 3 minutes.

Q6 Answer 45
Explanation: you must calculate the number of units of Product A sold in year 1 and subtract the sales of the following year from this figure. 5,000 x 30% = Product A year 1 sales, = 5,000 x 0.3 = 1,500. 1,500 – 1,455 = 45. 45 fewer units were sold in the following year.

Q7 Answer 800% increase
Explanation: you must find the percentage increase between 10,000 and 90,000. Start by calculating the increase 90,000 – 10,000 = 80,000. Now calculate 80,000 ÷ 10,000: cancelling zeros = 80 ÷ 10 = 8 x 100 = 800%.

Q8 Answer 62,500
Explanation: you must divide 1,250,000 by 20. You can do this quickly by first dividing by 2 and then moving the decimal point one place to the left. 1,250,000 ÷ 2 = 625,000, move the decimal point = 62,500.

Q9 Answer 9,000
Explanation: you must calculate 45% of 20,000. 20,000 x 0.45 = 9,000.

Q10 Answer 3 hours 57 minutes
Explanation: you must calculate 118.5% of 3 hours and 20 minutes. 3 hours and 20 minutes = 200 minutes, 18.5% = 0.185, 200 x 0.185 = 37, so the stopping train takes 200 + 37 = 237 minutes = 3 hours (180 minutes) 57 minutes.

Q11 Answer 1,200 gm
Explanation: you have to identify 40% of 3 kg and give your answer in grams (1 kg = 1,000 gm). 40% = 0.4, 0.4 x 3,000 = 1,200.

Q12 Answer 1/3
Explanation: this is simpler than it might seem. You have to find 1/2 of 2/3 = 1/3.

Q13 Answer 2 hours and 30 minutes

Explanation: first calculate when the plane did leave and then calculate the length of the journey. 13.40 + 55 = 14.35, 14.35–15.00 = 25 minutes, 15.00–17.00 = 2 hours, 17.00–17.05 = 5 minutes, = 2 hours 30 minutes.

Q14 Answer $9,250

Explanation: find the average or mean by adding the values together and divide by the number of values. 3,020 + 21,450 + 2,112 + 10,418 = 37,000 ÷ 4 = 9,250.

Q15 Answer 13 kg

Explanation: find 45% of 9 kg and then add it to 9 kg. 45% = 0.45 x 9 = 4.05, which is approximately 4, 9 + 4 = 13.

Q16 Answer 7 hours and 25 minutes

Explanation: 06.43–07.00 = 17 minutes, 07.00–14.00 = 7 hours, 14.00–14.08 = 8 minutes = total 7 hours and 25 minutes.

Q17 Answer 12%

Explanation: you do not need to know the size of the workforce to do this calculation, you must calculate the percentage decrease between 3.5 and 3.08. 3.5 – 3.08 = 0.42, 0.42 ÷ 3.5 = 0.12, 0.12 x 100 = 12%.

Q18 Answer 39 weeks

Explanation: 1 year = 52 weeks so you must calculate 75% of 52. 75% = 0.75 x 52 = 39.

Q19 Answer 40% loss of the original value

Explanation: 4,500 – 2,700 = 1,800, 1,800 ÷ 4,500: cancel zeros = 18 ÷ 45 = 0.4 x 100 = 40%.

Q20 Answer 1/5

Explanation: you must add 3/5 + (1/2 of 2/5) = 3/5 + 1/5 = 4/5 leaving 1/5 from other sources.

Q21 Answer 60%
Explanation: 57.6 – 36 = 21.6, 21.6 ÷ 36 = 216 ÷ 360 = 0.6 x 100 = 60%.

Q22 Answer Highest 27°, lowest 25°
Explanation: the mean is the average and the range the difference between the highest and lowest. Given a range of only 2 degrees the lowest must be one less than the mean and the highest one more.

Q23 Answer 126 hours
Explanation: there are 168 hours in a week, 7 x 24 = 168. You must calculate 75% of 168, 75% = 0.75 x 168 = 126.

Q24 Answer 48
Explanation: you have to add 1/3 and 2/5 and then calculate the remaining fraction of 180. 1/3 + 2/5 = 5/15 + 6/15 = 11/15 leaving 4/15 to be sold. 4/15 of 180 = 180 ÷ 15 = 12 x 4 = 48.

Q25 Answer 74.4 seconds or 1 minute 14.4 seconds
Explanation: you must calculate 93% of 1 minute 20 seconds. 1 minutes 20 seconds = 80 seconds, 93% = 0.93, 0.93 x 80 = 74.4 = 1 minute 14.4 seconds.

Q26 Answer 12 hours and 5 minutes
Explanation: the meeting lasted 2 hours and 25 minutes = 145 minutes x 5 = 725 minutes = 12 hours and 5 minutes.

Q27 Answer 3%
Explanation: 4,635 – 4,500 = 135: you must find 135 as a percentage of 4,500. 135 ÷ 4,500 = 0.03 x 100 = 3%.

Q28 Answer 45 minutes
Explanation: one hour = 60 minutes. You can add the two percentages 30 + 45 = 75 so you must calculate 75% of 60. 75% = 0.75 x 60 = 45.

Q29 Answer 11°

Explanation: you must find the mean or average, and you need the range and either the highest or lowest temperature to do this. Eg 14 ÷ 2 = 7 + 4: the mean temp = 11.

Q30 Answer 7 minutes

Explanation: you must add 4 hours and 17 minutes to 07.50 and work out how long after 12 noon this is. 7.50 + 4 hours = 11.50 + 17 minutes = 12.07 so it is 7 minutes late.

Q31 Answer 3,660 metres

Explanation: you must calculate 20% of 18.3 km and give your answer in metres. 18.3 kg = 18,300 m, 20% = 0.20, 18,300 x 0.20 = 3,660.

Q32 Answer 8% loss

Explanation: total revenue = 16,200 – 1,200 = 15,000. You must find 1,200 as a percentage of 15,000. Cancel zeros to get 12/150, divide top and bottom by 3 = 4/50 = 8/100 = 8%.

Q33 Answer 60%

Explanation: 8 – 5 = 3 days: you must find 3 as a percentage of 5. 3 ÷ 5 = 0.6 x 100 = 60%.

Q34 Answer 17/40

Explanation: you must add 1/5 and 3/8 and calculate the remaining fraction. 1/5 and 3/8 = 8/40 + 15/40 = 23/40 leaving 17/40 of the workforce travelling more than 30 minutes.

Q35 Answer 9 hours and 46 minutes

Explanation: calculate the time between 08.05 and 18.30 and subtract the time spent on taking the call and at lunch. Total 10 hours 25 minutes – 39 minutes = 9 hours and 46 minutes.

Q36 Answer 24
Explanation: calculate the number of women working for the company and then the number in the senior positions. 2/3 x 360 = 360 ÷ 3 = 120 x 2 = 240, 1/10 x 240 = 240 ÷ 10 = 24.

Q37 Answer 75%
Explanation: you have to calculate the percentage decrease between 16 and 4. 16 – 4 = 12, 12 ÷ 16 = 0.75 x 100 = 75%.

Q38 Answer 450
Explanation: first find 1/4 of the total and then 3/8 of that figure. 1/4 x 4,800 = 4,800 ÷ 4 = 1,200, 3/8 of 1,200 = 1,200 ÷ 8 = 150 x 3 = 450.

Q39 Answer 75%
Explanation: first calculate 2/3 and 1/6 of 60: 2/3 = 60 ÷ 3 = 20 x 2 = 40, 1/6 = 60 ÷ 6 = 10, so the decrease was from 40 to 10 minutes. Calculate this as a percentage decrease: 40 – 10 = 30, 30 ÷ 40 = 0.75 x 100 = 75%.

Q40 Answer 37.5% decrease
Explanation: first convert the ratios to decimals and then calculate the percentage decrease. 1: 5 = 0.2, 1:8 = 0.125. Now calculate the percentage decrease: 0.2 – 0.125 = 0.075, 0.075 ÷ 0.2 = 0.375 x 100 = 37.5%.

Test 2 Sequencing

Q1 Answer 1
Explanation: these are the factors of 21: 1x21, 3x7, 7x3, 21x1.

Q2 Answer 56
Explanation: add 8 to the previous sum at each step beginning with 8 x 6 = 48.

Q3 Answer 63

Explanation: 168 (– 7x6=42), 126 (– 7x5=35), 91 (– 7x4=28), 63 (– 7x3=21), 42.

Q4 Answer 112

Explanation: 69 (+ 21), 90 (+ 22), 112 (+ 23), 135.

Q5 Answer 156

Explanation: add 12 to the previous number at each step beginning with 12 x 11 = 132.

Q6 Answer 4

Explanation: 12 (– 8), 4 (– 7), –3 (– 6), –9

Q7 Answer 24

Explanation: 79 (– 5x6=30), 49 (– 5x5=25), 24 (– 5x4=20), 4 (– 5x3=15), –11.

Q8 Answer 50

Explanation: divide the previous number by 50 each step: 2500÷50 =50.

Q9 Answer 0

Explanation: subtract 7 from the previous number at each step in the series beginning with 7x3=21.

Q10 Answer 31

Explanation: this is a part of the series of prime numbers starting at 23.

Q11 Answer 99

Explanation: 264 (– 6x11=66), 198 (– 5x11=55), 143 (– 4x11=44), 99 (– 3x11=33), 66.

Q12 Answer 222
Explanation: 222 (+ 99), 321 (+ 100), 421 (+ 101), 522.

Q13 Answer 0.04
Explanation: divide the previous number by 5 at each step: 0.2÷5=0.04.

Q14 Answer 60
Explanation: subtract 6 from the previous number at each step beginning with 6x10=60.

Q15 Answer 110
Explanation: add 11 to the previous number at each step beginning with 8x11=88.

Q16 Answer 70
Explanation: 81(– 11), 70 (– 12), 58 (– 13), 45.

Q17 Answer 344
Explanation: 344 (– 5x12=60), 284 (– 4x12=48), 236 (– 3x12=36), 200 (– 2x12=24), 176.

Q18 Answer 5
Explanation: these are the factors of 15: 1x15, 3x5, 5x3, 15x1.

Q19 Answer 41
Explanation: 45 (– 2x2=4), 41 (– 2x3=6), 35 (– 2x4=8), 27 (– 2x5=10), 17.

Q20 Answer 317
Explanation: 8 (+ 102), 110 (+ 103), 213 (+ 104), 317.

Q21 Answer 256
Explanation: divide the previous number by 4 at each stage: 1024÷4=256.

Q22 Answer 40

Explanation: subtract 8 from the previous number at each stage beginning with 8x8=64.

Q23 Answer 70

Explanation: add 7 to the previous number at each stage beginning with 10x7=70.

Q24 Answer 18

Explanation: 21 (– 2), 19 (– 1), 18 (– 0), 18.

Q25 Answer 30

Explanation: 84 (– 6x4=24), 60 (– 6x3=18), 42 (– 6x2 =12), 30 (– 6x1=6), 24.

Q26 Answer 10

Explanation: these are the factors of 10: 1x10, 2x5, 5x2, 10x1.

Q27 Answer 91

Explanation: 36 (+ 27), 63 (+ 28), 91 (+ 29), 120.

Q28 Answer 125

Explanation: multiply the previous number by 25 each step: 5x25=125.

Q29 Answer 77

Explanation: subtract 11 from the previous number at each step beginning with 7x11=77.

Q30 Answer 30

Explanation: add 3 to the previous number at each step beginning with 3x8=24.

Q31 Answer 99

Explanation: 300 (– 100), 200 (– 101), 99 (– 102), –3.

Q32 Answer 99
Explanation: 99 (– 7x3=21), 78 (– 6x3=18), 60 (– 5x3=15), 45 (– 4x3=12), 33.

Q33 Answer 216
Explanation: this is 6 raised to the powers 6^2, 6^3, 6^4, 6^5.

Q34 Answer 25
Explanation: 14 (+ 11), 25 (+ 12), 37 (+ 13), 50.

Q35 Answer 0.4
Explanation: multiply the previous number by 2.5 at each step: 0.16x2.5=0.4.

Q36 Answer 0
Explanation: subtract 9 from the previous number at each step beginning with 9x3=27.

Q37 Answer 60
Explanation: add 12 to the previous number at each step beginning with 12x4=48.

Q38 Answer 99
Explanation: 99 (– 30), 69 (– 29), 40 (– 28), 12.

Q39 Answer 27
Explanation: 72 (– 5x5=25), 47 (– 5x4=20), 27 (– 5x3=15), 12 (– 5x2=10), 2.

Q40 Answer 6
Explanation: these are the factors of 24: 1x24, 2x12, 3x8, 4x6, 6x4, 8x3, 12x2, 24x1.

Test 3 Data interpretation

Sales of bullion by the ounce and the sums raised

Q1 Answer $87,000

Explanation: you must multiply 290 x 300. Do this quickly by calculating 29 x 3 = 87 and then adding the 3 zeros to get 87,000. Don't forget the $ sign and to show your answer as $87,000 not $87.

Q2 Answer 150

Explanation: you must divide 40,950 by 273 (40,950 was raised from the sale of an unknown number of units at a unit price of $273).

```
     150
    ------
273 | 40950
    | 273
    | 1365
    | 1365
       0
```

Q3 Answer $275

Explanation: you must divide 68,750 by 250.

```
     275
    ------
250 | 68750
    | 500
    | 1875
    | 1750
    | 1250
```

Q4 Answer $277
Explanation: to find the average total the four prices and divide by 4, 270 + 275 + 273 + 290 = 1,108 ÷ 4 = 277. Do not forget the $ sign.

Q5 Answer $4,000
Explanation: in 2000, 200 units were sold at $270. Had they been sold in 2003 they would have raised $290 each, $20 more per unit. So 200 x 20 = $4,000 more would have been raised.

Expenditure of a small manufacturing company

Q6 Answer 29%
Explanation: you must add 8 + 3 + 18 = 29.

Q7 Answer $360,000
Explanation: you must calculate 40% of 900,000 = 900,000/100x40. Cancel zeros to get 9,000 x 40 = 9 x 4 plus 4 zeros = 360,000.

Q8 Answer Materials and premises
Explanation: materials = 32% and premises 18%, these are the only two items that added together total half the expenditure.

Q9 Answer 144°
Explanation: the pie graph = 360° so you must find 40% of 360, = 360/100 x 40 = 3.6 x 40 = 144.

Q10 Answer 4 : 5
Explanation: you must simplify 32:40. Both are divisible by 8 (8x4=32, 8x5=40) so they simplify to 4 : 5 (this means that for every $4 spent on materials $5 is spent on wages).

Extracts from a financial statement for a small business

Q11 Answer $880,250

Explanation: the figures from 2003 show that value of sales are obtained by adding cost of sales + gross profit, for 2004 = 668,990 +211,260 = 880,250.

Q12 Answer ($5,000)

Explanation: subtract the administrative expenses from the gross profit to find the operating profit, for 2003 = 169,218 – 174,218 = –5,000. Show the loss by placing the figure in brackets: ($5,000).

Q13 Answer False

Explanation: Sales dropped between 2003 and 2004, so the improvement was achieved by other means.

Q14 Answer True

Explanation: you do not need to calculate each percentage to answer this question and in a real test you might not have time to. Sales decreased but gross profit increased so the percentage must have improved. If you require greater certainty then modify the sums to make them more convenient and to speed up the calculation.

Q15 Answer False

Explanation: you have to find if 27,000 is more or less than 3% of 880,250. Save time by making the calculation more convenient by estimating 27 as a percentage of 880 = 1% of 880 = 8.8 x 3 = 26.4. You should now see that 27,000 as a percentage of 880,225 is greater than 3%, so the statement is false.

International tourists worldwide and by region

Q16 Answer 2

Explanation: you can see from the table that only Africa and Europe saw an increase. (If you answered 4 regions then you might have mistakenly read the table from left to right when the dates are the other way round.)

Q17 Answer 0%

Explanation: if you add up the five regions' % shares they total 100%. From this you can infer that according to the table the remainder of the world received no share of world tourism.

Q18 Answer Middle East

Explanation: The Middle East % share fell from 2 to 1 which is a 50% drop; Asia saw the next biggest drop from 15 to 10 (33%).

Q19 Answer 4.8%

Explanation: Add 0.6 + 7.5 + 14.5 + 2.6 = 25.2 – 1.2 (the negative growth for Asia) = 24, then divide by 5 (the number of regions) = 4.8. Don't forget the % sign.

Q20 Answer False

Explanation: as a percentage of worldwide tourism the Middle East share has decreased but the question does not ask this. The number of tourists visiting the Middle East has increased by 2.6% a year so in real terms the number has increased.

Pie graphs comparing employment by industrial sector in two regions

Q21 Answer 7%

Explanation: the whole pie graph = 100%. Subtract the given sums to find the remainder. 33 + 37 + 10 + 8 + 5 = 93, 100 – 93 = 7% for construction.

Q22 Answer True

Explanation: these sorts of business are tourist-related and Region 1 has a greater percentage of workers employed in this sector. It is therefore reasonable to conclude that there are more of these sorts of business in Region 1.

Q23 Answer 2,000,000 or 2 million

Explanation: 800,000 = 2% and you must find 5%. 800,000 ÷ 2 = 400,000 = 1%, 400,000 x 5 = 2,000,000.

Q24 Answer Cannot tell

Explanation: the size of each workforce is not given, only their relative sizes as a percentage of the whole. It is therefore not possible to tell which region employs the most people, only that a greater proportion of all those employed in Region 1 work in tourism.

Q25 Answer 120°

Explanation: a pie chart = 360°. The percentage employed in retail and distribution = 33%, 33% = 1/3 = 360/3 = 120°.

Indicators of development

Q26 Answer Cannot tell

Explanation: the populations for the countries are not given so you cannot calculate the number of doctors per country, only the ratio between doctors and patients.

Q27 Answer 2

Explanation: this can be readily read off the table: country 3 = 10, country 4 = 12, 10 – 12 = 2.

Q28 Answer 4:1

Explanation: the birth and death rate per 1,000 for country 1 = 46 : 11.5 which simplifies to 4:1 (11.5 x 4 = 46).

Q29 Answer Cannot tell

Explanation: only the rate for (all) deaths is given so the rate for the death of infants cannot be calculated.

Q30 Answer Country 3

Explanation: population increase is the difference between birth and death rate (when immigration and migration are excluded). The question asks you to identify the slowest-growing population. This excludes country 4 as its population is decreasing. So this means the answer is Country 3, as its population is growing at a rate of 10 – 8 = 2 per thousand.

Monthly average levels of rainfall and temperature for three regions of Europe

Q31 Answer B

Explanation: the temperatures enjoyed by region B are significantly higher than the other two regions and these higher temperatures are enjoyed for longer.

Q32 Answer A

Explanation: Region A experiences the lowest temperatures.

Q33 Answer C

Explanation: the temperatures for Region C best fit this description as they range between 3° and 15°, avoiding the higher temperatures experienced by Region B and the lower temperatures of Region A.

Q34 Answer A

Explanation: precipitation means rain. By comparing the graphs it can be seen that region A experiences the most rainfall.

Q35 Answer A

Explanation: the temperature range for region A is between below zero and 20°, making the range approximately 21°.

Gender and age cohort of a population

Q36 Answer Women

Explanation: it is clear from the graph that the female population makes up a greater percentage of the total population aged 65 and more.

Q37 Answer False

Explanation: the narrow base suggests the opposite, namely a smaller proportion of young people as a percentage of the total population.

Q38 Answer 15–64

Explanation: if you study the list of different age groups it is clear that the range of the middle cohort is 15–64 years.

Q39 Answer 4%

Explanation: you must total the percentages given for both male and female children of these ages. Female 0–4 1%, female 5–9 1%, male 0–4 1% and male 5–9 1% = 4%.

Q40 Answer Long

Explanation: a population structure for a country with a short life expectancy would taper as the population aged. This population structure is relatively straight, suggesting a long life expectancy.

Interpretations of your scores

Chapter 1 quick tests

A score of over 65%

This is the level of score you should aim to realize in these quick tests in order to be sure that you have the speed and accuracy necessary to succeed in numeracy tests. These quick tests examine your command of the key mathematical operations tested in every numeracy test. A high degree of competency in these key operations will serve you well. While other candidates are recalling their basic maths you will be performing these basic calculations much more quickly and without error, so you will gain important seconds, make fewer mistakes and be better able to focus on the questions and avoid the traps that test authors so like to set.

A score over 50%

This is a good score but it could be better! If you failed to complete all the questions in the time allowed, then keep practising to build up your speed. Go over the test and identify which questions you got wrong, and concentrate your practice on these operations. Keep practising and after a few hours of hard work you will notice the improvement. Then do more and you will soon be up to full speed.

Work through all five of the quick tests found in Chapter 2 and set yourself the personal challenge of getting a better score in each test. Remember that to do well in a test is a matter of hard work and determination, so really go for it.

A score below 50%

Let maths become something of a preoccupation and work at it in most of your spare time. Consider obtaining more practice questions than are contained in this book. I have suggested suitable sources at the start of most chapters.

Go over the questions that you got wrong and concentrate your efforts on these operations. If you failed to attempt sufficient questions in the time allowed, revise the multiplication tables again and take the next test determined to attempt more questions than in the last test.

Revise the key operations until you can answer the quick test questions almost without thinking. It might take some time but you will succeed in mastering these fundamental skills. It might be boring, painful even, but with hard work you will do it.

Multiplication tables

Learn them.

X	1	2	3	4	5	6	7	8	9	10	11	12
1	1	2	3	4	5	6	7	8	9	10	11	12
2	2	4	6	8	10	12	14	16	18	20	22	24
3	3	6	9	12	15	18	21	24	27	30	33	36
4	4	8	12	16	20	24	28	32	36	40	44	48
5	5	10	15	20	25	30	35	40	45	50	55	60
6	6	12	18	24	30	36	42	48	54	60	66	72
7	7	14	21	28	35	42	49	56	63	70	77	84
8	8	16	24	32	40	48	56	64	72	80	88	96
9	9	18	27	36	45	54	63	72	81	90	99	108
10	10	20	30	40	50	60	70	80	90	100	110	120
11	11	22	33	44	55	66	77	88	99	110	121	132
12	12	24	36	48	60	72	84	96	108	120	132	144

Conversions between fractions, decimals and percentages

You should know these off by heart.

Decimal	Percentage	Fraction
0.05	5%	1/20
0.1	10%	1/10
0.125	12.5%	1/8
0.2	20%	1/5
0.25	25%	1/4
0.3	30%	3/10
0.375	37.5%	3/8
0.4	40%	2/5
0.5	50%	1/2
0.75	75%	3/4

Adding and subtracting negative numbers

Replace double signs with a single sign using the following rules:

Replace + + with +
Replace – – with +
Replace + – with –
Replace – + with –

Realistic tests chapter 6

A score over 30

This is a good score and you can expect to do well in a real test of your numeracy skills. If you face a graduate psychometric test or a test for a managerial position, this is the only score you can afford to be content with.

In the Kogan Page testing series you will find more realistic tests and questions at the advanced level in *How to Pass Advanced Numeracy Tests* and *The Advanced Numeracy Test Workbook*, both by Mike Bryon.

A score of 20 or above

Most candidates who take a numeracy test will gain a score in this category. Keep practising to be sure that you get a positive result in a real test where your performance might be adversely affected by nervousness. Go over the questions and explanations that you got wrong and the fundamentals that were involved. Continue practising these operations until you are confident that you have mastered them. Keep working to improve your mental arithmetic.

In the Kogan Page testing series you will find further suitable practice questions in the following titles: *How to Pass Numeracy Tests*, 2nd edn, by Harry Tolley and Ken Thomas; *How to Pass Numerical Reasoning Tests* by Heidi Smith; *How to Pass Selection Tests* by Mike Bryon and Sanjay Modha; and *The Ultimate Psychometric Test Book* by Mike Bryon.

A score below 20

Continue to extend your efforts to revise your mental arithmetic. Consider undertaking one hour's practice every day over the next month. When travelling on a bus or train, or when out for a walk, pose and answer simple sums for yourself. I knew a determined candidate who purchased a large number of revision textbooks intended for children, containing page after page of questions using the basic operations. (You can purchase them in many bookshops.) He worked on these for weeks until his speed and accuracy were greatly improved. He was then able to take his basic maths for granted and concentrate instead on evaluating the data presented and the numerical reasoning that the question required. Try it; you have absolutely nothing to lose and everything to gain.

Go over the questions that you got wrong and use the explanations to help you realize where you have been going wrong.

If you failed to complete enough questions in the time allowed, keep practising to build up your speed.

Don't give up. Just keep practising. You will get better but it takes hard work and determination!

Further reading from Kogan Page

Interview and Career Guidance

The A-Z of Careers and Jobs, 13th edition, Susan Hodgson, 2006
Careers and Jobs in IT, David Yardley, 2004
Careers and Jobs in the Media, Simon Kent, 2004
Careers and Jobs in Nursing, Linda Nazarko, 2004
Careers and Jobs in Travel and Tourism, Verité Reily Collins, 2004
Choosing Your Career, 2nd edition, Sally Longson, 2004
Great Answers to Tough Interview Questions, 6th edition, Martin Yate, 2005
How You Can Get That Job, 3rd edition, Rebecca Corfield, 2002
Odd Jobs, 2nd edition, Simon Kent, 2002
Online Job Hunting, Martin Yate and Terra Dourlain, 2002
Preparing the Perfect CV, 4th edition, Rebecca Corfield, 2007
Readymade CVs, 3rd edition, Lynn Williams, 2004
Readymade Job Search Letters, 3rd edition, Lynn Williams, 2004
Successful Interview Skills, 4th edition, Rebecca Corfield, 2005
The Ultimate CV Book, Martin Yate, 2002
The Ultimate Interview Book, Lynn Williams, 2005

The Ultimate Job Search Letters Book, Martin Yate, 2003
Your Job Search Made Easy, 3rd edition, Mark Parkinson, 2002

Titles in the Testing Series

The Advanced Numeracy Test Workbook, Mike Bryon, 2003
Aptitude, Personality and Motivation Tests: Assess Your Potential and Plan Your Career, 2nd edition, Jim Barrett, 2004
The Aptitude Test Workbook, Jim Barrett, 2003
Great Answers to Tough Interview Questions: How to Get the Job You Want, 6th edition, Martin John Yate, 2005
How to Master Personality Questionnaires, 2nd edition, Mark Parkinson, 2000
How to Master Psychometric Tests, 3rd edition, Mark Parkinson, 2004
How to Pass Advanced Aptitude Tests, Jim Barrett, 2002
How to Pass the Civil Service Qualifying Tests, 2nd edition, Mike Bryon, 2003
How to Pass Firefighter Recruitment Tests, Mike Bryon, 2004
How to Pass Graduate Psychometric Tests, 2nd edition, Mike Bryon, 2001
How to Pass the New Police Selection System, 2nd edition, Harry Tolley, Billy Hodge and Catherine Tolley, 2004
How to Pass Numeracy Tests, 2nd edition, Harry Tolley and Ken Thomas, 2000
How to Pass Numerical Reasoning Tests, Heidi Smith, 2003
How to Pass the Police Initial Recruitment Test, Ken Thomas, Catherine Tolley and Harry Tolley, 2004
How to Pass Professional Level Psychometric Tests, 2nd edition, Sam Al-Jajjoka, 2004
How to Pass Selection Tests, 3rd edition, Mike Bryon and Sanjay Modha, 2005
How to Pass Technical Selection Tests, Mike Bryon, 2005
How to Pass Verbal Reasoning Tests, 2nd edition, Harry Tolley and Ken Thomas, 2000
How to Succeed at an Assessment Centre, 2nd edition, Harry Tolley and Robert Wood, 2005
IQ and Psychometric Test Workbook, Philip Carter, 2005
Test Your Own Aptitude, 3rd edition, Jim Barrett and Geoff Williams, 2003

CD ROMS

Psychometric Tests, Volume 1, The Times Testing Series, Editor Mike Bryon 2002

Test Your Aptitude, Volume 1, The Times Testing Series, Editor Mike Bryon, 2002

Test Your IQ, Volume 1, The Times Testing Series, Editor Mike Bryon, 2002